RACIAL ORIGINS OF
ENGLISH CHARACTER

RACIAL ORIGINS OF ENGLISH CHARACTER

WITH AN APPENDIX ON LANGUAGE

BY

R. N. BRADLEY

KENNIKAT PRESS
Port Washington, N. Y./London

RACIAL ORIGINS OF ENGLISH CHARACTER

First published in 1926
Reissued in 1971 by Kennikat Press
Library of Congress Catalog Card No: 72-118461
ISBN 0-8046-1210-2

Manufactured by Taylor Publishing Company   Dallas, Texas

PREFACE

A BOOK on racial origins of character must necessarily comprise both deductive and inductive elements. To write of character requires personal observation, whereas in dealing with racial origins considerable research is necessary, for which one is in the nature of the case largely dependent on the work of others. That must be my excuse for drawing so freely on the writings of Mr Harold Peake, Professor Fleure and, to a lesser extent, of Lord Abercromby. The book, however, is not a mere popularization of the works of these authors. The views herein set forth are merely a development of ideas which appear, more or less in embryo, in *Malta and the Mediterranean Race* and *Duality*. That they now approach finality is due largely to Mr Peake, who has in his detailed account of the steppe-folk, the men of the Leaf-Shaped Sword, supplied a missing ethnological link.

I have a more definite debt to acknowledge to Mr E. M. Forster and the publishers, Messrs Edward Arnold & Co., for permission to quote a very picturesque paragraph in chapter xvi. from *A Room with a View*.

For including a philological appendix I have a precedent in Sir John Rhys' *Welsh People*, in which Professor Morris Jones gave an account of Hamitic or African syntax in Welsh. Like most truths it was still-born, yet it was no more than half a truth. He found the right syntax but the wrong language. The steppe-folk who as the Gaels introduced Indo-European speech to these islands were ultimately of African origin and brought an African language. It is therefore useless any longer to search for explosive Aryan and Asiatic roots to account for our language ; this came from Africa or nowhere. I show how it could have emerged only as Arabic, the proto-Semitic language, and, before the reader turns away with a shrug, I will ask him one question. Suppose we started *de novo* without any preconceptions, to which theory would we give credence in the following instances : that *waist* means the part where size and strength are developed, where the body *waxes*, as Skeat would have it, or that it means *middle*, as in Arabic ; that *lad* means " one who is led," or that it is the regular shortening of *walad*, a boy ; that *soot* is so called because it *sits*, or because it is *black*, this being the Arabic meaning of the word ? To the unprejudiced, given the necessary basic arguments, there can be no doubt.

R. N. B.

MEADWAY COURT
July 1926

CONTENTS

RACIAL ORIGINS OF
ENGLISH CHARACTER

CHAPTER I

THE BASIS OF INQUIRY

ENGLISH character has formed the subject of many volumes, chiefly of foreign origin, wherein the Englishman has been dealt with, humorously, satirically, appreciatively, or from the naïve point of view of his appeal to the stranger. Apart from sarcastic pleasantries on the subject of our hypocrisy, Sabbatarianism, lack of humour, the studies have often been of a serious nature and, both from the French and the American side, we have met with considerable praise. For an Englishman to be either loosely sarcastic or, on the other hand, merely laudatory in dealing with his own people would be barely pardonable and, although both praise and blame will be discovered in these pages, it is hoped that they will be found dispassionate, *sine ira et studio*, and solely illustrative of characters which are based on scientific foundations. I cannot help feeling that so much light has recently been thrown on our racial origins that a study of this nature should not only be useful, but is required.

Racial studies of our people have hardly proceeded

beyond a contrast between Celt and Saxon and, as these are ethnologically almost the same people, the basis of comparison needs some revision. Who are Celts ? Are they Welsh, Irish, Highlanders, Low-landers, Cornish or Bretons ? All can lay claim to the appellation, and yet there is little in common, except a kindred language, between the Welsh Methodist and the Highland gillie. It is a case where language has been misleading and, though the first Indo-Germanic speech must have been brought to these islands in the form of Gaelic by probably fair-haired Nordic leaders, and Welsh came later with Belgæ of similar appear-ance, what remains of this ethnological type among the Celts of Scotland, Ireland or Wales ? The speech was that of the leaders, who were few, and they not only brought with them soldiery and settlers of another race, but they settled among an indigenous people, who not only survived but still probably form the great substratum of the population. For this reason it is probable that Celtic speech in our islands mainly represents a constant pushing westwards and northwards of the earliest settlers, speaking a tongue bequeathed to them by a few conquerors who were, at an early date, swallowed up in the population. These earliest settlers were mainly of the Mediter-ranean Race, Hamitic in origin, and are a relic of an early invasion from North Africa which gave the human race a new start, while at the same time gathering up the relics of the palæolithic peoples. Of this type were the short dark Silures of South Wales, representatives of at least one phase of this migration ; and the fact that in spite of numerous invasions we tend to revert almost uniformly to the dark long-headed type indicates how important is the Hamitic substratum in our islands.

We shall have to deal with various ethnic currents, but broadly they have two directions, northward from Africa and westward from Asia. The conflict of the long and the round skull, of the Hamitic and the Mongol type, seems to have begun before neolithic times, for in Cro-Magnon man of the Magdalenian epoch we trace Mongolian features and a race blend. Evidences of Asiatic penetration are found in early Egypt accompanied by the introduction of metals. A very early Lappish culture runs across the North of Europe and seems to penetrate through Britain to Ireland, and may account for the earliest settlements in that island. The difference between the two types is so wide that theory has, at times, tended in the direction of ascribing three cradles to the human race and to trace the white man to the chimpanzee, the Mongol to the orang-outang, and the negro to the gorilla. In any case the differences in language, character and in certain somatic features seem to be so fundamental between the Hamite and the Mongol that it is, in many respects, difficult to assign to them a common origin. Dr Crookshank in *The Mongol in Our Midst* shows how the hospital Mongol is a reversion to the racial type and in the direction of the orang-outang, whereas *dementia præcox* is another form of reversion towards an Egyptian type and the chimpanzee. These phenomena take place in our midst; if they are truly racial reversions, and the supposition is not improbable, it is apparent that we have among the English far wider distinctions to consider than the division of Celt and Saxon, but that within our shores we have racial variations as wide as humanity itself.

We are called English, taking our name from the Angles, who were only a section of the contemporary invaders. Professor Ridgeway finds some distinction between Angles and Saxons in the important matter of burial, but these differences between the Eastern settlers and the rest are swallowed up in more important racial differences of earlier occurrence. The Anglian half of our country is also the half in which the earlier Beaker-folk left their traces which, despite various waves of Nordics, inhere in the characters of the present inhabitants. Nordics in the guise of Gaels, Britons, Saxons, Angles, Jutes, Danes and Normans have invaded our shores since the coming of Beaker-man, without in a great degree disturbing his sphere of influence, and this may in some measure be accounted for by the fact that the earlier Nordics came associated with short-headed Alpines who were racially akin to the Beaker type. In the Eastern counties, therefore, the short-headed Beaker type has been reinforced. If we can judge from Sussex it would appear that some at least of the Saxons came as an unmixed type, and hence it came about that the West of England is more long-headed than the East. There is still another feature tending to enhance this division in that the Alpines who accompanied the Nordics were of a peaceful and industrial disposition and tended to remain where they first settled, refusing to adopt a life of conquest and adventure. These considerations lead to a broad division of our people into the old Anglian section embracing Bernicia, Mercia, East Anglia and Kent on the one hand, and the part to the west of these territories on the other.

The Nordics, somewhat broader-headed than the Mediterraneans, are nevertheless of the long-headed type and represent a development and probably some admixture. The cumulative effect of the various movements has been to emphasize short-headed and Asiatic character in the East, and the long-headed and Mediterranean in the South and West. Such racial divisions explain the saying that the East-coast fisherman follows the fish while the Devonians wait for the fish to come to them ; why Yorkshire is Liberal and Lancashire essentially Conservative ; why the Roundheads drew their support from the Eastern counties and the Lowlands of Scotland ; the rivalry of neighbouring counties like Warwick and Worcester ; and many religious and political as well as somatic differences.

The following chapter will show how our characters were influenced mainly by Mediterranean, Beaker, Alpine and Nordic origins and tradition, and these are the names which occur most frequently in this study. There are older types and newer invaders. The latter are but repetitions, and their influence is less in that they came at a time when our people was more settled and less plastic, for it is the impressions and experiences of childhood which mould the people no less than the man. Of very ancient types Dr Fleure has been able to find evidences in the moorlands of Wales, appropriate refuges for primeval man. Such types, Neanderthal perhaps, Cro-Magnon more certainly, may well be imbedded in our people, but their importance would be more individual than general and they would have little bearing on the study of English character.

CHAPTER II

HISTORICAL FOUNDATIONS

THE comparison of the characteristics of long- and short-headed man is full of interest, which increases with the evidence recently brought into prominence of the fundamental differences between the two, pointing possibly to distinct cradles of the race and, in the opinion of some, separate lines of descent from pre-human ancestry. With these differences pervading both history and psychology I have dealt elsewhere, and, in doing so, have been obliged to isolate the characteristics to a degree which is not altogether consonant with the mixed condition of most present-day peoples.

It is now necessary to consider certain mixtures and modifications which are important from a racial point of view, and it is possible to do so the better in that the question has in recent years been very adequately dealt with by Mr Harold Peake and Dr Fleure, two anthropologists who have filled many of the gaps in the ethnology of these islands. It is superfluous to follow the utmost ramifications of early European races. Modern man appeared in North Africa about 15,000 B.C. and was distinguished by the culture called Capsian. Invading Europe at several periods he appears to have swallowed up

various remnants of the Palæanthropic period, notably
Grimaldi and Combe Capelle man. All three types
were long-headed, that is, their skulls were long from
back to front. Grimaldi man belonged to Western
Europe, was prognathous and negroid and may
account for small dark types in Apulia and Sardinia,
while he probably formed the basis of the South
Welsh. The Combe Capelle type had high, narrow
heads, protruding upper jaws, retreating foreheads,
broad noses and sharply marked brow-ridges. Combe
Capelle man had always, before the Capsian invasion,
been a raider and horse hunter, had invaded Central
Europe, and had driven the tall, artistic Cro-Magnon
men to the Pyrenees.

Capsian man invading Central Europe at some
period from 7000 to 6000 B.C., and swallowing up or
driving out earlier inhabitants, represents the long-
headed Mediterranean race of Sergi.

About 6000 B.C. another current of humanity set in
from the Western Himalayas, the short-headed Ofnet
people, who combined with Combe Capelle remnants
to form the Alpine Race. The mixture caused a
certain lengthening in the front of the skull, but
the Alpines remain a short-headed race, though not
so brachycephalic as Ofnet man. According to Mr
Peake, fresh waves of the Ofnet race brought a
knowledge of grain, cultivation of fruits and domesti-
cation of animals, and eventually the Alpines evolved
the pile-dwellings of Switzerland and Northern Italy.
It is interesting to observe how the two original races
of Sergi, the Eurafrican and the Eurasiatic, are vin-
dicated by later research ; but there are still many

crossings, alliances and interweavings to be considered before we can account for modern peoples.

In the neolithic period—taking for example the
megalithic culture of Malta of about 3000 B.C.—
emerges a new type who appear as leaders of the
Mediterranean race.   There is a movement of culture
from the Eastern Mediterranean through Crete,
Malta, Spain, Brittany, the West of France, to the
British Isles, and it is associated with the dolmen
and these new leaders, to whom has been given the
name of *Prospectors*. This newly discovered type
affects me with a vague misgiving, but there appears
to be nevertheless widespread evidence of its existence.
The *Prospector* is dark, strongly built and broad-
headed, the *Etruscus Obesus* of the ancients, and is
said to be found to-day in maritime towns and cities,
Venice, Genoa, and fishing villages in Ireland and
Wales.   By some the great Minos of Crete is assigned
to this type, no less than the tyrants of Greece,
merchant princes ousting Nordic tribal kings, like
Leverhulmes in our House of Lords.

I cannot say from my knowledge of Malta that I
am unfamiliar with the type, though broad-heads
appeared to me to be rare in Malta.   But I am somewhat at a loss in associating *Prospectors* with such a
purely religious thing as the dolmen-stream.   Crete,
Malta, Carnac, Dartmoor, in their ancient manifestations suggest nothing practical or mercatorial, and
yet who shall maintain that in Malta of to-day, teem-
ing with churches and priests, one is in the midst of
religious idealists ?   In Ireland the Catholic priest is
often a shrewd business man, and so perhaps in ancient

times no little business ability was mingled with devotion to ritual. Yet we feel that these ancient Prospectors were not of the type of a Leverhulme or a Cadbury, nor do I think we need greatly differentiate them from the later Phœnician merchants who consolidated their trade routes by establishing depôts on a line reaching to our own islands.

Though the desire for gain is deeply embedded in the Mediterranean Race, they are not by nature a roving people. The Greek navigator hugs the coasts, and the Maltese is an unwilling colonist.˙ The phenomenon of these people in their early days wandering as far as Ireland and making settlements on the way seems almost incredible unless they were subject to some special impetus, and I cannot help conceding to Minoan Crete just that dash of Asiatic blood which Sir Arthur Evans would assign to its rulers. It is more than possible that in so far as the Mediterraneans were adventurers they were so in virtue of some such extraneous leadership or admixture. But on the whole it seems more possible to accept the view that, the long-headed people being already well established in Europe from ancient days, the dolmen and the long barrow represented a culture-spread rather than a definite racial movement. As to the dark brachycephals in Welsh and Irish sea-port towns and villages, I find it difficult to believe that a small Anatolian element should have crystallized out after so many centuries, for the dolicephals are noted for their power of absorption. From examples I have seen among the well-to-do Maltese I should incline to the view that they are a development within the

Mediterranean Race itself. Dr Fleure says that the head tends to broaden with greater infant care, and nowhere is this more likely to be found than among merchant princes.

Partly as a result of well-being, partly owing to infiltration from the East, these dark brachycephals seem to have developed out of the Mediterranean Race, while the dolmens, as I show later, are an indication not only of religious but of commercial activities.

We now come to two peoples who vitally affected our character and history, the Beaker-folk, and the Steppe-folk ; and, whatever we may have known about them before, our information was of a vague and general nature, and it is owing to Mr Peake that they are fitted like jig-saw fragments into the historical picture. The former were originally the Tripolje folk, a broad-headed race with prominent, but not continuous brow-ridges, who pursued a peaceful culture on the Eastern side of the Carpathians. By their broad heads they must be related in some way to the Alpines or Ofnet people, but the affinity has not been worked out. Taller than the Alpines and less brachycephalic they may be a cross between Alpine and Nordic, or Ofnet and Combe Capelle. They lived in pit-dwellings, burnt their dead and painted their pottery. Whence their beakers came is a matter of some doubt, both Galicia and Bohemia having been suggested, while their famous bell-beaker is said to have originated in Andalusia. A mixed race may easily carry on the traditions of several lands and here we have probably an instance. Their coming to

our shores and subsequent wanderings in Britain, so
minutely described by Lord Abercromby, seems to
have been due originally to a drought which un-
settled the world and brought their neighbours, the
steppe-folk, upon them.

The last named now materialize as the great invaders
of history and only by a perusal of Mr Peake's *Bronze
Age and the Celtic World* can adequate justice be done
to them. They are the old Kurgan people of Russia
who buried their dead in a contracted position in
barrows and painted their remains with red ochre,
customs which hark back to the Mediterraneans.
They were tall dolichocephals and have long been
known to us, though in a vague manner, as the
Nordics. A slight broadening of the head combined
with an independent, fearless and roving disposition,
argues a slight Asiatic admixture. We can imagine
a nomadic tribe, like Abraham's, wandering off northwards, absorbing new blood, and acquiring courage
and recklessness in the dangers of exploration, striking
the rich pastures of South Russia, living on the land
so long as it kept them and their herds, and then
moving off to new fields when the old were exhausted.
Probably the original tamers of the horse, they lived
a wild rodeo-like existence as cow-boys and rough-
riders ; they are indeed the ancestors of the Roman
equites and our own cavalry regiments. To-day our
high-brows call them Philistines and may be speaking
more truly than they know. The Philistines, or some
of them, came from Crete, the home of the earliest
rodeos. Widely disseminated in Palestine, which
takes its name from them, they had " the straight nose,

high forehead and thin lips of the European." It would not surprise me if they turned out to be the forefathers of the Nordic Race.

After expelling the Tripolje folk they wandered to Thessaly and Thrace and took the second city of Hissarlik. So closely were they associated with the horse that Mr Peake thinks they gave rise to the legend of the centaurs. They founded a dynasty in Mesopotamia and it has been surmised that with an Alpine admixture they helped to form the Hittites.

Mr Peake has traced their later wanderings by the disposition and development of their leaf-shaped swords over a period stretching from 1500 B.C. to 875 B.C., when the swords merge into those of the Hallstadt culture. At first their weapons were of bronze and it was as a bronze-sword people that they established themselves in Greece as the Achæans, and spread in other guises to Italy, Britain and Ireland. Afterwards a branch of them having learnt the use of iron in the Caucasus returned to Hungary, their centre of dispersion, and set out again on a second career of conquest with swords of the new metal, and invaded Greece about 1000 B.C. as the Heraclids or Dorians.

From Northern Italy they drove out the pile-dwellers, Alpines probably mixed with their own cousins of the bronze sword, and these pile-dwellers are supposed by Mr Peake to have founded a new city at Rome as a *terramara* on the Palatine Hill.

In due course this iron-sword people became predominant in Italy and in France except the Seine region.   They appear in this migration to have reached neither Britain nor Scandinavia.

Mr Peake's most interesting and valuable contribution lies in the new aspect thrown on the division between the *q*- and the *p*-Celts, those who said *equus* or *quatuor* and those who said *hippos* or *pedhair*—the Gaelic and the Cymric branches.   The *q*-folk were the bronze-sword men and the *p*-folk these of the iron sword.   Those who first brought a so-called Indo-Germanic language to our shores were Gaelic-speaking *q*-Celts, while France was overrun by *p*-Celts, the Sequani of the Seine provinces alone retaining the *q*-speech.

These various convulsions had their influence in our islands.   The first had the effect of sending us the Tripolje Beaker-folk who landed about 2000 B.C. and, occupying our uplands, pursued one course up the Eastern side of England to the North of Scotland, and another through Berkshire and across Salisbury Plain.

About 1150 B.C. followed the disturbers of the peace, the bronze-sword men themselves, tall, fair, long-headed, driven out by the iron-sword warriors, but Mr Peake thinks they came as officers, bringing a short-headed Alpine soldiery in their train, and this is a most important point to remember in considering the foundations of English character.

Later Celtic invaders, the Gauls or Belgæ, entered France about 400 B.C., driving out a *Crannog* or pile-dwelling folk who took refuge at Glastonbury and Mere in Dorsetshire.   In turn came the Belgic invaders themselves, a tall, fair, rather broad-headed race, whom we must suppose to be Nordics with a strongish Alpine admixture, and they are supposed to have constructed our hill-top or contour camps as at Malvern or Chanctonbury. About 300 B.C. the Cymri, descendants of the iron-sword *p*-Celts, invaded Britain and were afterwards driven to Wales in the time of Aulus Plautius.

Subsequent historic invasions by Angles, Saxons, Jutes, Danes and Normans do not materially affect the problem. They are all types of Nordics, more or less mixed with Alpine blood. Superimposing themselves upon our population and institutions they did not materially alter our racial elements in the country except that they had the effect of strengthening somewhat the Nordic strain. As regards our national institutions and national character however they were extremely important in making the Nordic outlook predominant above all racial sentiments.

After surveying these many invasions it is important to consider what are their effects upon race, character and institutions, and it is essential to remember that a change in psychology and customs may be altogether disproportionate to the numerical strength of the reformers. The most virile of our invaders, the Nordics, appear to have come as a minority of officers to the armies of Alpines, and yet it was the Nordic culture that prevailed. We see something of the same conditions in Greece and Rome, where the culture was that of the Patrician minority, and in Feudal Europe, where the culture of the lord stamped itself upon nations ; the most outstanding case is that of the Roman Empire itself. It will be well to consider the racial results first, and those more transcendental aspects afterwards.

Let us review the various types, past and present, associated with these islands. There is the Piltdown skull, palæonthropic, a brutish type nearly related to the chimpanzee ; and the remains of Galley Hill man, more developed but yet far from the civilized human being. These types did not persist except sporadically and may therefore be left almost out of account. Then comes the Tilbury skull and ancient crania of the river-drift, the earliest relics of modern man and, though thousands of years old, yet not differing materially from those of the modern Londoner. These may be at least equated with the Capsian men of North Africa who appeared about 12,500 B.C., if they are not actually Capsians. In time they become merged in the long-headed Mediterranean Race.

Dr Fleure's *Anthropological Types in Wales* puts us in touch with various isolated racial remnants. In the Plynlimmon uplands are found a long-headed type bearing features older than Neanthropic, heavy brow-bridges, low and sloping foreheads, massive and retreating lower jaw, all characteristic of Neanderthal man. Here on those inhospitable heights a remnant of one of the oldest races may have sought refuge and maintained certain racial characteristics, despite interblending, until modern times.

The short, long-headed Picts of Northern Scotland and the Silures of South Wales we may set down as typical Mediterraneans. It is interesting to remember that predominant among the ancestors of the Mediterranean Race are the Combe Capelle people with high narrow heads, prominent brow-ridges, broad noses, and with the upper jaw projecting over the lower. The last character is often seen among the English and, in fact, distinguishes the caricature-Englishman of continental illustrations. It is somewhat difficult to isolate this feature from the well-known adenoid jaw, which dentists tell us arises from the habit of sucking the thumb or the use of comforters in babyhood. But just as there are racial Mongols and pathological Mongols, so there may be more or less permanent forms of adenoid jaw. Nature progresses by these accidents and is apt to crystallize them. I know instances of this alveolar prognathism, as it is called, which is certainly racial; for instance in my own family we run in two types, the one being very dolichocephalic, dark, Mediterranean and possessing this form of prognathism; the other more brachycephalic with higher cheek-bones, a trifle ruddier, and with normal jaws. My mother assures me that we were all equally well, or badly, brought up.

Another component of the Mediterraneans, the Grimaldi type, were entirely prognathous, without brow-ridges, small and negroid in character. The type is found in Sardinia, Apulia, and is not absent from our islands; it may form the basis of the South Welsh.

In Wales, too, notably along the Bala gap which was on the trade-route to the Irish gold-fields, we find broad-headed men, taller than the neolithic Mediterraneans, with strongly marked though not continuous brow-ridges; these are the Beaker-men, and Mr Peake thinks they represent our intellectuals. The Darwins are certain of this type and Sir Oliver Lodge and the late Lord Salisbury also seem to belong to it. It has to be remembered generally that the broad-head is the intellectual head, while the long head tends to be emotional or instinctive.

Little to be distinguished from the Beaker-folk are the brachycephalic Alpines, who are supposed to be a cross between the Ofnet race and Combe Capelle. With the characteristics of the Swiss and the tall stature produced by cross-breeding they have had great influence on our national character, although their head-shapes have tended to be absorbed by the Mediterranean type.

In various coastal towns and villages of Wales, especially Newquay, we find nests of the so-called *Prospectors*, tall, dark broad-heads, generally fisher-men, once associated with the dolmen-stream. They seem to correspond to similar settlements on the Leinster coast and probably indicate trade-routes with Ireland. In character they are said to be distin-guished by business ability.

The Nordic is well known to us, being our best public-school type, reminding us of Mr Aldous Huxley's phrase, " Nature's Guardsmen." Tall, blue-eyed, fair-haired, courageous, chivalrous, he has always been the darling of our lady novelists, which means that sexual selection has gone in his favour. He is the backbone of our character and institutions, and to describe him must necessarily occupy the greater part of this book. He first invades us as the man of the leaf-shaped sword ; he was then probably Gaelic speaking, and he has since been reinforced on many occasions by Saxons, Danes and Normans. The Saxons and the

Scandinavian invaders of the Scottish coasts were of the purest Nordic type ; the Jutes and Angles, judging from their descendants, are both more brachycephalic in head-shape and more Asiatic in character.

There is still another type which crops up at intervals and seems to be a throw-back to something primitive, and that is the Mongolian type—short of stature, with a broad square head, high cheek-bones, very dark hair and eyes, and with the eye-sockets square and raised high at the outer and upper angles. Those who have an opportunity to compare, especially in the Pitt-Rivers Museum at Oxford, typical dolicephalic and brachycephalic skulls will observe that the set of the eye-sockets is entirely different in the two cases ; in the brachycephal they are not only square, but squarely set.   Professor Elliot Smith, who has studied the question exhaustively in Egypt and elsewhere, notes also that the brachycephals are distinguished by a broader and shorter ramus of the jaw, which gives the face a squarer and firmer appearance. These are characteristic differences between African and Asiatic man, and in Egypt the coming of the Giza people is a clearly defined Asiatic infiltration.

In a recent work, *The Mongol in our Midst*, Dr Crookshank has collected much useful information as to those sporadic Mongols.   The hospital Mongol was originally so called because of his resemblance to the racial Mongol.   The writer gives evidence as to the markings on the hands of these deficients, their adoption of the cross-legged Buddha position in sitting, their general mentality, all in addition to the more ordinary Mongolian traits, which tend to indicate not only a hereditary descent from the racial Mongol, but a strong relationship with the orang-outang. In another form of deficiency, *dementia præcox*, the patient adopts what is called the Egyptian position, squatting on the hams with the legs in front of him, and the arms at rest symmetrically in front. This form of deficiency seems to hark back, through the Mediterraneans, in the direction of the chimpanzee. In these two maladies, which seem to be due to atavism owing to weakness of the parent stock, we seem to find some foundation for the mythical figures of Japhet and Shem. Ham apparently finds his affinities in Neanderthal man and the gorilla ; but it must be remembered that the Ham spoken of is the black man, the negro. In scientific ethnology the Hamites are not necessarily black, but include the ancient Egyptians, the Libyans, always characterized by a tendency to blondness, and other North African peoples, who are in fact representatives of the Mediterranean Race.

Apart from pathological cases, Mongolism is preserved in various nests in Europe, notably Brittany, and may be a relic of the Ofnet race or of other Asiatic elements.

While some of the Asiatics blended with indigenous folk to form the Alpines, others seem to have continued unmixed and with them is associated the Maglemose culture, the Kitchen-middens of Denmark, and later the Campignian culture which passed over Scotland to Ireland, bringing to the latter its earliest settlers, wretched beach-dwellers, whose remains are chiefly shell-heaps and rude stone huts.

I think this early immigration of Mongoloids from

Scandinavian lands has not been treated with the attention it deserves, for it seems to explain some of the characters of the " old Irish," the tinkers of the West, with their short heads, tip-tilted noses and mischievous eyes ; it may account for instances of Mongolism springing up in the region of Lancashire—Cuchullain himself seems to have been one of these people ; it may explain a certain Mongolism inherent in the Welsh ; and more especially very noticeable Ugrian tendencies in the Welsh and Irish languages. The Bretons are markedly Mongoloid and this may be due to immigration from Britain or to local Asiatic remnants, or both. The Nordic is free of Mongolism, but it is possible that any brachycephals are prone to revert to it, quite apart from Maglemose influence.

We gather from *The English Village* of Mr Peake that the earliest system of cultivation in England was the Valley Village under the three-field system ; at a later date came the moorland and forest cultivations under the one-field system. The reason for the latter is that the moorland and forest cultivations arose out of the pastoral habits of the invading Nordics. Mr Peake thinks that agriculture was first brought to England by the Beaker-folk, who introduced a perfect moorland-village community. To them he ascribes the terraces which we still see upon our Downs. From Lord Abercromby's account of the migrations of these Beaker-men I am a little doubtful about ascribing so much to them. They were few and poor and, although they seem to have been good thrifty stock, I cannot help thinking that a great deal was going on before their arrival. Those who have examined, at first hand, the prehistoric monuments of a station like Malta are astonished at the density of the neolithic population and its comparatively high state of civilization, and I am inclined to the view that the Mediterranean population and culture were predominant in Britain long before the coming of the Beaker-folk. It is an acknowledged fact that the broad substratum of our population is of the Mediterranean type, and it could hardly be the prevalent type to-day if it had not been so before the numerous invasions of more or less Asiatic peoples. The Beaker-men were brachycephalic ; the Nordics, long-headed but less so than the Mediterraneans, are supposed to have brought with them numerous brachycephalic Alpines ; the Saxons were mixed in the same way, and so were the Normans ; the Danes had probably a stronger brachycephalic admixture than either. And yet to-day, as Ripley points out in his *Races of Europe*, the English are a one-race type ; in the Beaker-men the breadth of the head was eighty-three per cent of its length, but with the British to-day it is pretty uniformly seventy-seven to seventy-nine per cent. We know that the long-headed type is both persistent and absorbent, and it seems quite clear that the brachycephalic elements have been absorbed and that the population has reverted. But it would not have reverted unless there was a numerous stock to which to revert.

If Stonehenge is a Bronze-Age monument, there are numerous relics of earlier date. The culture of the Long Barrows, with the chambered tomb and the semi-circular forecourt, have features in common with remains in the Balearics, Sardinia, Malta and North Africa. Similarities in customs, the prevalence of the spiral and other ornaments, relics of villages, standing stones, remains of sanctuaries, vestiges of prehistoric roads on Dartmoor and elsewhere, all closely paralleled by those of Malta ; numerous and detailed similarities of this kind seem to leave little doubt of the spread of a Mediterranean civilisation.

The argument could be clinched in a very effective manner if there was an accepted theory of neolithic language ; in the absence thereof we seem to be ploughing the sand. Archæologists point to the old names of our rivers and other physical features which they suggest must give the key to the primitive language of our islands. Those who are interested in the subject are referred to the Appendix, which I think should clear up many of our doubts.

The first Indo-Germanic language brought to these shores appears to have been Celtic of the *q*-type, namely Gaelic, and it was probably introduced by the Nordics, although it is not impossible that the Beaker-folk brought some such speech. Then what of the names of rivers and natural features which are unexplained by Celtic ? This is the mystery before which all our authorities are dumb.

The Appendix shows that the main vocabulary of Indo-Germanic speech is Arabic ; and I may go further and say that these old river names like *Thames*, *Swale*, *Nidd* and *Tees* are Arabic also. This is no hare-brained Orientalist theory, for Arabic is the language which should have been looked for in the first instance. It is the language of prehistoric Malta, a stronghold of the Mediterranean Race, and whereas we might expect the persistence of a Hamitic language from North Africa—and indeed Professor Morris Jones found traces of Hamitic syntax in Welsh—the fact remains that it was not Hamitic which survived among us. Arabic developed out of Hamitic, and Hamitic syntax, perpetuated in Arabic, found its way into Welsh.

The Nordics, originally Mediterraneans, nomads like Abraham, were originally bedouins. And despite their admixture with Asiatics the old speech seems to have survived with them though causing some difficulty as it spread to unaccustomed lips.

But many of our place-names appear to be pre-Nordic, and if that is so, in so far as they are Arabic, they point to the fact that Arabic was spoken in Britain before the arrival of the Indo-Germanic languages. A few pure Arabic words like *heifer*, found only in these islands, together with the persistence among us of certain Arabic shibboleths like *th*, tend to corroborate this view.

It is supposed that the Beaker-folk brought some of their pottery originally from Spain, and indeed it is conceivable that they bore with them our neolithic culture, but as Lord Abercromby calculates that they originally landed some four hundred strong, it hardly seems probable.

If an early Mediterranean culture in these islands can be conceded we are faced with the probability of conditions, not indeed comparable with those of Crete, but possibly analogous to those of prehistoric Malta. Leaving aside the Mediterranean character for a time we can judge pretty well from Maltese remains of the kind of culture this would be. Crowded round megalithic sanctuaries on moorlands near the sea would be the rude stone dwellings of the populace. A great part of their life would be devoted to religious observances, in shaping and ornamenting their sanctuaries, in setting up stones for ceremonial purposes and for the guidance of pilgrims to the shrines. The visitors came not empty-handed, and in time the sanctuary became a market and the roads to the sanctuary trade-roads. The market came to be held at the period of the feast, just as the Breton *pardons* are also fairs. They were a sea-people and preferred to keep in view of their element. The Isle of Wight and Dartmoor would be ideal sites for them, and they preferred a chalk locality for the sake of the flints obtainable.

Perhaps we can now get a glimpse of the significance of the Prospectors. There was undoubtedly a coastwise traffic over a route extending from the Eastern Mediterranean to Ireland, and it was probably carried on by these Prospectors, men possibly with a dash of Anatolian or Sumerian blood, somewhat akin to the folk they traded with, and yet of superior courage and originality. If the Mediterraneans lived near the sea, and if their festivals tended to develop into markets, we can quite understand how great dolmen-centres and megalithic sites like Carnac in Brittany became associated with Prospectors, for the dolmen cluster meant a great market and maritime emporium, keeping the old folk in touch with their ancient home and traditions, as well as serving the more useful purpose of exchange.

Mr Peake is inclined to ascribe some at least of our water-meadow culture to an Alpine strain in the iron-sword folk, but those who know the Salisbury district with its Mediterranean associations of nomenclature and populace would be more ready to associate this form of cultivation with folk from the Mediterranean regions, the home of irrigation ; irrigation words bulk largely in the vocabulary taken over from Arabic.

We may perhaps grant that the Asiatics brought a knowledge of corn and fruits and their cultivation, disseminating this culture from Central Europe. Such useful knowledge must have been spread beyond the confines of the Alpines. And though the influence of both the Beaker-folk and especially the Alpines must have been great in these islands, it seems probable that its importance lay in character and method. The Beaker-men, notable for their intellect, doubtless brought system and knowledge to bear on social and domestic problems. The Alpines, more numerous and better equipped, were probably able to transport their culture bodily ; forced originally for the purposes of safety to become lake-dwellers, they learnt from the exigencies of their cramped and artificial villages the necessity of co-operation, of social help and mutual sacrifice, and acquired those qualities of individual anonymity which characterized both the Roman and the Republican Swiss. This co-operation was the essence of early village systems and doubtless gave them vigour and permanence.

I do not think it would be correct, however, to allow these considerations to overshadow entirely an earlier Mediterranean culture which must not be considered negligible, and a further consideration of Malta may give us some inkling of its nature. The tendency of the neolithic Mediterraneans was towards matriarchy, a fact which may be due to a somewhat developed and certainly a peaceful culture. Traces of matriarchal descent are found among the Picts and elsewhere in this country. There was no farming or pasturing on a large scale ; we must rather imagine rude cultivation in small plots around the habitations, a dependence to some extent upon shell-fish and the products of the sea ; domestic or semi-domestic animals, chiefly goats or sheep, would be kept but probably on a miserable scale ; possibly animals were hobbled then as they are in Mediterranean countries to-day. There would be some hunting and trapping of wild birds and animals. In fact the present day conditions in rural Malta or Sicily may be taken as roughly representative of our pre-Beaker culture.

In *The English Village* Mr Peake gives numerous hints on the origins of our character and institutions which we cannot afford to neglect, however much we may expand the subject later. The relation of Nordic lord and Alpine follower has laid the foundation of our politics, history and national character. We have here the hunting, shooting squirearchy who ride straight and speak the truth, the foundation of our Conservative party, on the one hand, and, on the other, the trader and shopkeeper class who later develop dissent and Liberalism, the finest type being the Quaker. The element of disciplined social co-operation seems to have been enhanced in our Alpines by the Danish invasion, whence may come the tendency towards trades-unionism, although I myself doubt it, largely for the reason that these sturdy short-heads were able by force of character and by orderly living to raise themselves above the scope of trades-unionism before it came into force. Whatever the idea may owe to the Asiatic brachycephals its prevailing tone is largely Mediterranean, reminding one not a little of the market-place of Athens. Trades-unionism is for the poor, and the Alpines are not poor.

Our Nordics have always displayed a certain individualism which Mr Peake ascribes to the isolation of Scandinavian farmsteads. More especially have they always upheld the cause of freedom, whatever that may mean, since social philosophers say that it can have no meaning. It is necessary to ask, they say, Freedom to do what ? For just as one man's meat is another's poison, so is any man's freedom to do a thing an obligation upon all others to let him do it. To a Nordic lord this presented no difficulties, but it makes one wonder whether our greatest upholders of British freedom did not envisage a freedom for themselves at the expense of many others who never entered into their calculations.

Whereas the Alpines became dissenters, re-echoing the sentiments of prophets and reformers in Alpine lands, we are told that Methodism, a Church of England revival, appealed to the Nordic heath-dwellers made outcast by the enclosures of the lords. And while many Alpines will be found among Methodists, a survey of Hampshire or Sussex with their chapel-strewn heaths will, I think, lend considerable conviction to Mr Peake's view in this repect.

CHAPTER III

NORDIC CHARACTER

WHATEVER be the preponderance of blood in our veins there can be no doubt about the standard English character, which is as well known to ourselves as it is to foreigners. When we say that a thing is not English there is no uncertainty in our minds nor in our hearers' as to what is meant. " English " connotes numerous qualities both physical and moral—such things as personal cleanliness, cold baths, a fondness for games and sports, a code of honour and truthfulness in speech. Yet although all may aim at this high standard, there are really few who can afford to live the typical English life, which is the life of a country gentleman. The ideal, if not the typical, Englishman must have the advantage of a public school education ; sometimes he goes to the 'varsity, but this is inclined to introduce variations which are not typical. The public school turns out a type, but the 'varsity turns out, if not individuals, little groups of individuals characterized by some eccentricity—religion, good works, drinking, asceticism, art or psychics. In a way it is our salvation.

The type is not learned and has not much use for learning. At school the " swot " is not popular—certainly he is not typical. There is a gulf fixed between the Army and the Civil Service, the respective homes of good form and of learning. It came as a surprise to me years ago when I discovered the contempt which was poured upon distinguished scholars in the Civil Service by military men. I thought a university record would count for something and would entitle the holders to some respect not only from the point of view of learning but of status. This was a fundamental error. The university has a religious and monastic tradition : it was the home of " clerks " or clerics and, whereas the clergy are nowadays respected, at least in the established church, there was a time when a priest was kept like a house-dog in our stately homes. Recently I stayed at a house which had a little ancient square erection in the garden like a long box standing on end ; the ground floor was the private chapel, and on the upper floor the priest was kept. He ascended to his kennel by a ladder. The clergy were expected to have learning as one of their points, but in their masters it was regarded as an eccentricity.

The squire of the old days was the typical Englishman, fond of horses and of drinking, dealing out rough justice on the bench, charitable to his tenants and underlings provided they kept in their proper places ; attending church as a matter of form ; sleeping in the sermons ; persecuting dissenters ; hating radicals ; living a normal, moral, regular life ; essentially a man of character in that you could prophesy what he would do on any occasion. His sons went into the Army or Navy ; the eldest inherited the estate and the youngest sometimes went into the Church. He was a healthy, active, out-of-door man, always doing something, and never bored ; chivalrous to women, but determined to keep them in their proper place, as good wives or daughters ; he would tolerate no feminine antics.

To-day the type is more widely disseminated. Many of the old estates are broken up and the descendants of the ancient families have taken to trade, but the old manner and the old accent survive. Though they have not the old background, the types familiar to Mr Stephen Mackenna are still distinguishable if only by their imitations.

That these are pseudomorphs is only too obvious, and the pain that they cause is mitigated by the consolatory reflection that this pseudomorphism has, despite our racial mixture, perpetuated the Nordic spirit. Soon after the Great War I heard a bank-clerk inveighing against the officers of a certain regiment who followed the well-known British custom of finishing their bacon-fat by mopping it up with bread on the end of a fork. His listeners, time-honoured ladies of a private hotel at Southsea, were duly disgusted, but the sentiment sounded to me like pseudomorphism of the wrong kind. The officers were doubtless good soldiers and brave men, and probably fought better by virtue of the bacon-fat, which is after all particularly nourishing and had a great war-time value. But the fact that a bank-clerk should be so impressed by their breach of etiquette only shows how strongly certain customs, particularly affecting the partaking of food, are ingrained in our national character.

It is the Nordic custom to dine in the evening, the

Alpine to dine at midday ; late dinner is accordingly a mark of good form. The triumph of the ideal over the practical is particularly Nordic and English. It seems to hark back to the customs of the hunting field where you are not out so much to kill your fox as to kill him in a certain way. The Mediterranean is only out to kill him, and Brigadier Gerard made a *faux pas* in this direction.

There is a Nordic etiquette with regard to animals. William Rufus loved the red deer as if he were their father, and the Nordic loves the thing he kills, or rather the thing he sets apart for his killing. He divides animals into game and vermin or, as it were, Nordics and Alpines, or Nordics and Dagoes. The game animal has certain rights, and must be killed only in a certain way and by certain people. The man who shoots a fox is himself degraded to the status of vermin.

I used once to fish a stream where I was constantly running up against a very fine angler and champion caster. He dealt very lovingly with his trout and you might almost think they would regard it a privilege to die at his hands. Then one day I saw him kicking and mauling a large fish most unmercifully—it was a chub who had dared to take his fly.

Readers of Mr W. H. Hudson will remember the wanton cruelties which used to precede the slaughtering of cattle in South America. The Mediterranean is brutal to animals and loves to torture them. It is as if he suffered from an inferiority complex and worked it off on dumb beasts, or perhaps it is the cruelty of infantilism in which the feelings of others are not

realized. But it is very different with your Nordic :
his cattle, his pigs may be destined for the butcher,
but till then how he loves them, with what pride he
regards them ! His love even extends to the butcher.
It is not that he is very much more humane, but
he recognizes certain conventions. He is the inventor
of the game with its recognized rules, and the animal,
or at least the patrician animal, came within the
purview of those rules.

He is never foolish enough to be a vegetarian or to
join societies for prevention of cruelty to animals, for
he would not recognize any feelings or considerations
outside the rules. He could never admit that the
rules were wrong ; that is left to transcendental
spirits, life's vagabond prophets, who are often enough
developed Mediterraneans ; for these, knowing no
rules, often make new ones of their own and so become
leaders or wreckers of humanity. It was reserved for
one of their race to say : " I have not tasted my fellow
creature for twenty years." And it is sayings like
these that make a man like Bernard Shaw anathema
to the Nordic. Once when I was living in an English
Cathedral city I seized the advantage of seeing his
Pygmalion acted by a touring company. Fired by
my praise some other guests in the house, including a
temporary major and country gentleman, followed my
example. On the return of the party the officer was
asked by an Air Force chaplain and his wife how
he liked the play. " Filthy, disgusting, horrible ! "
he said ; " how anyone can listen to such filth I can't
understand," with a severe glance at me. " Yes, I
thought as much," said the chaplain's wife, shrugging

her shoulders, while the chaplain put the seal of the Eternal on the proceedings. This ignorant prejudice is typical of racial manifestations. But to the seeker after light and reason it is perhaps a matter for congratulation that the Great Race is in some measure passing.

For the Nordic loves neither brains nor intellectualism. Clever talk either frightens or bores him, and his public school education certainly does not cause hypertrophy of the brain lobes. It is a rough-and-tumble where sport and character count, and where one learns to put up with hardships without complaining. Parents may know that food is short and bad, and that various unnecessary hardships have to be borne, but they also are imbued with the Nordic spirit and pay out enormously and with Spartan fortitude for the sake of the code.

In religion the Nordic, being not untouched by racial mixture, favours a compromise. Just as he is originally a Mediterranean so his church is founded on the old Catholic Church of the Mediterraneans, but his egotism enables him to maintain that this unrecognized offspring is older than the parent. At Salisbury, among other places, I have heard it seriously maintained that the Church of England is the original church as founded by St Peter and that the Catholics split off owing to " errors " ; and a certain Dean, preaching in one of the old churches taken from the Catholics, was bold enough to call on the very stones of which the church was built to witness the permanence and continuity of Anglicanism from the earliest Christianity.

The ritual of the Church of England is eminently suitable to the character of our Nordics, being formal, dogmatic and illogical, yet orderly and of a routine nature. It has sloughed off those sensuous aids to worship, such as incense, images and pictures, which are so essential to the more emotional Mediterranean. For the priest and the Pope, who are persons outside the pale of nationality, it substitutes a parson or person indeed, but he is an Englishman, who is known to them, who dines at their table, whose sons are in the Army or Navy, and who is, generally speaking, a Nordic first and a priest afterwards. We know that when attempts were made to introduce Christianity to the old Nordics of the continent, Christ had to be disguised as a fierce warrior leading his troops. With us a different compromise is made. Christian doctrine is read in our churches, but in such a formal and routine manner that the sense is glozed over ; Christianity is not inculcated, but its reverse, namely, snobbishness and exclusiveness ; and perhaps rightly. For Christianity is no religion for the Nordic, and it breaks down at once as soon as he comes to deal with subject peoples. If he treats them as equals, as his Bible tells him he should, his empire vanishes in smoke.

But he needs some form of religion mainly for disciplinary purposes and Christianity serves as well as any other so long as it is only treated as a formality. And the form adopted is, like the Nordic himself, half-way between intellectual, doctrinaire, presbyterian Alpinism, and sensuous Mediterraneanism. It requires compliance without absolute submission, and allows a certain limited freedom to the individual. And while it asks for no unreasoning childlike faith, it does not, on the other hand, require any deep thought or effort of the intellect such as are demanded by a Scottish sermon. It is the Church of Rome and Italy, as modified by the Alpines, Luther, Calvin and Zwingli.

The Nordic is naturally a leader and an officer, but it is possible that like England herself he is living in some degree on the heritage of the past. At his first coming he was a natural superior in many ways; tall and strong, he was an athlete, trained by his nomadic existence to ride, kill, harry and conquer. His patriarchal mode of life had fostered male domination, while the nature of his existence had necessitated recognized leadership and succession; migration and forays demanded organization, councils, and some specialization, but above all they required a band of fighters and workers who were willing to take orders. The Nordics came as a privileged and commanding class, and this position they have in some degree held ever since.

A class in such a position, when life becomes normal and easy, necessarily tends to degenerate, since the qualities which created it are not brought into exercise. The Nordics seem to have been fully alive to this, and the " spiritual discipline " which has been ascribed to the English may in some measure be due to a fear of deterioration. Keenly aware of their heritage, they have not only partaken fully in public activities, but have kept their minds and bodies fit by constant exercise, and fostered their military qualities by sport. In the last respect the mantle of the Romans has fallen upon them ; the proverbial connection between Eton and Waterloo is comparable to the relation between Roman games and the Roman army. The discipline of the cold bath, of floggings and hardships at school, of dangerous games, of long days spent in hunting and shooting on little food, so incomprehensible to the practical Latin, has a psychological background of a mission of military leadership.

Nevertheless, changing conditions have left their mark on Nordic character. The position, being one of status, has come to depend on status, and the Nordic occasionally, but not always, cuts a poor figure without his retinue and entourage. It is useless to command if there is no one to take orders, and difficult to obtain recognition on one's merits if no one knows who you are. It is for this reason that the English gentleman may cut a poor figure in European circles. His wonted domination, his sports, his muscles, go for nothing, and his lack of brainpower and contempt of foreign languages and customs place him at a disadvantage. Of late years, however, he has learnt that other countries do exist otherwise than as lands to be conquered and, whereas he was always respected, or at least envied, for his wealth and character, he now tends to be less unpopular. Nevertheless the person who has done most for our popularity abroad is not the gentleman, but " Tommy Atkins."

I once read a case where a famous judge, noted for his debonair manner in court, was openly defied by a defendant, some dancer or other who did not know the conventions. One saw then how much his position was dependent on status and tradition. When this was no longer recognized he seemed to be utterly at sea, and the case made very poor reading. It seemed to typify the weakness of the Nordic position, which is apt to rely on convention rather than on reality.

Another circumstance which has gone against him has been the growth of commerce and the competition of foreign countries. In a commercial struggle with Germany internal status is of no utility, and brains and business ability have been required. He chafed under pre-war conditions and in his heart was not sorry that the arbitrament was left to the sword and not to brains and hard work. His spirit, trained in war, is apt to be a danger in peace, for in permeating our culture it makes itself felt in commerce, with the result that status rather than efficiency is looked to there for a remedy. If our industry cannot compete with the foreigner, whereas the Scot will improve his efficiency, the English are apt to ask for a tariff, as if English goods should triumph of right and not on their merits. Moreover, it is in our commerce that a certain inherent weakness of intellect and lack of education are manifest ; we still live on the heritage of Alpines or Beaker-men like Adam Smith or Mill, for few of our business men are capable of understanding Political Economy. We have been saved again and again from disaster as if by miracle and it is difficult to understand how. It seems we have to thank the working-man and the banker for buttressing the commercial position of which many commercial men do not seem to grasp the elements.

The first Nordics have been reinforced in this country in various ways, by Angles, Saxons, Norsemen and the later Normans, but the nature of the reinforcement has varied. It would appear that the Normans came very much as the first Nordics came, organized as Lord and Vassal, and some of the old Saxon lords were ousted and reduced. Angles and Saxons came as more homogeneous bodies of settlers, and between them there seems to have been a slight racial difference, for the Anglian counties remain different from the Saxon, more Puritan and Asiatic and, before the conquest, Angles and Saxons tended to band together against each other. The Saxons appear to have been typical Nordics of a fairly homogeneous character, or at least so we should judge from their settlements. Sussex is a county where the Saxons have been somewhat isolated, and it is interesting to analyse the character of its people. Typically they are tall, fair-haired and blue-eyed, and of ruddy complexions. There is about them a certain softness which characterizes the Saxon generally ; they are genial, kindly, good-natured, somewhat deliberate, open-hearted, hospitable and cheerful. There is a feeling of well-being and happiness in Sussex which you do not find among the indigenous peoples of Kent or Hampshire. If the people are prone to Methodism it has to be remembered that the Nordic, dispossessed by the Enclosure Acts, found consolation in this revival. His dissent is, however, less emphatic than that of Wales. And if the Sussex man has been reduced to farmer and labourer, you see from his bearing that he is still a Nordic and, despite his humility, he has a deep, exclusive pride. An old Sussex woman was talking, with some disgust, to my mother about her grandson, who had left the country and gone North. " Fancy him," she said, " a Sussex lad, a-wastin' of hisself in the Sheres ! " You will note the delicate insinuation that England consists of Sussex and the Shires. Similarly an old man was telling my brother of a trip to London which he made on the invitation of his son. He described all the wonderful experiences and my brother asked him whether he would not like to go again. " Oh, no," he said, " Old England's good enough for me." In this case the position of Sussex is magnified still further. Its people have a pride of place and birth and long tradition ; government, orders, improvements, progress are regarded with quiet contempt. " I've never done this rationin' yet," said an old Sussex woman to my mother during the war, " and I ain't a-goin' to begin now."

Devon, too, is an ancient home of the Nordics, and no better examples of the true Nordic character can be found than Drake and his associates. Its spirit of free-lance adventure regarded the world as a field of conquest and all that sailed the seas as free game, yet it was not without a code of honour and morality, a special conventional code of its own. These characters, combined with an absence of general plan, a coolness in danger, a contempt of odds, and a high carelessness, show these men of Devon to be true descendants of the parent stock. In Devon, too, may be found among the women the best types of Nordic beauty, with fresh complexions, wavy hair, blue eyes, oval faces with regular features. But the county has a very large substratum of Mediterraneans and it may be for this reason that the population falls more and more into the grip of *dolce far niente*. Visitors from the North or East, while appreciating the hospitality, charm and geniality of the Devonians are, at the same time, struck by the pervading spirit of laziness and procrastination, the inability or unwillingness to grapple with the problems of the moment, which is characteristic also of the Irish. My sister used to amuse me with her experiences as a householder in South Devon, and one trifling tale links up with the Sussex anecdotes. It was also during the time of war restrictions, when food was severely rationed. My sister was visiting a farm in the county and went with the farmer's daughter to see her feed the fowls. She noticed to her surprise that the girl was throwing them the finest English wheat. " Oh," said my sister, " but you're not allowed to do that, are you ? " " No," drawled the girl in reply, " but we does." As a further mark of kinship, through the Mediterranean, with the Irish, the Devonian has a pretty if slower wit. There was a case in North Devon where two suspicious characters were haled before justice on a charge of smuggling, but were acquitted. A few people were discussing it with the local postmaster, who was also the village Whiteley. " And the judge said they left the court," said one, " without a stain on their character." " Oh," said the postmaster, " that's better than they was before then."

CHAPTER IV

ALPINE AND BEAKER CHARACTER

BEAKER-MAN is held to be an intellectualist and the Alpine an industrialist, but it is somewhat difficult to sort them out to-day. Darwin, with his shaggy eyebrows and overhanging ridges, is supposed to be a good example of the former, but both are probably a mixture of Ofnets with Mediterraneans ; the round skull predominates, while the Mediterranean strain is represented sometimes in the length of face. Beaker-man however probably had Nordic blood in his veins and by virtue of this he is taller than the Alpine. The Beaker-men landed in South-Eastern England and spread North and West from there, but are mostly found in the Eastern counties right up to the North of Scotland. The Alpines, associated with the Nordics, would have followed the progress of Celtic speech to both Scotland and Ireland, but it is probable that the farther they spread the more they became diluted with Mediterranean blood. They were settlers and workers and would probably not follow their conquering lords farther than they were obliged. The Eastern counties were nearer their source, and it is there that we mostly find them ; Kent, the Eastern counties proper, the old Mercia, ancient Bernicia and Deira, and the Lowlands of Scotland. We know them by their psychology ; the home of the Quaker-Puritan spirit is in the Eastern counties and Southern Scotland. You have only to visit Huntingdonshire to-day and in certain districts you will find almost every man a replica of Oliver Cromwell. There are sharp divisions in counties where the races march, as between Kent and Sussex, Warwick and Worcester, Yorkshire and Lancashire, the former of each pair inclining to Puritanism and Evangelicalism, dissent, Liberalism, industrialism, the second to Conservatism, orthodoxy, even Catholicism, agriculture and country pursuits. Lancashire is indeed industrial, but more by accident than by design ; it is a naturally conservative and agricultural county, and harboured the old faith long after it was dead in the rest of England.

It is not necessary to say much here about the Alpine type as it is continually touched on in a cursory way. We all know the characteristics of the Puritan and his descendant, the modern dissenter ; we all know and respect the Quaker. Some think it is a misfortune that Liberalism should be associated with cocoa, but it is a natural and racial association. The Quakers make cocoa, biscuits and many other wholesome things because they are descended from those old lake-dwelling communities who found themselves isolated among their enemies and were obliged to develop the social and therefore moral life for self-protection. Living in such close quarters induced a corporate responsibility, just as the isolated dwellings of the Nordics fostered individualism and a selfish outlook. With the Alpine it was necessary for each man to pull his weight, and it was advantageous to

help him to do so.   Each person's troubles were known,
and knowledge necessarily brought help, and this attitude remained when the community split up and
developed in the Quaker into an unparalleled altruism
in which all the world was his neighbour.   And, as
has been said, this close communal life allowed none
to be master, for that is impossible when each is too
well known.   The proverb that familiarity breeds
contempt is relevant here, and if none appeared worthy
of kingship, on the other hand, in the absence of a
desire for war, the need for kingship did not arise.
And thus was evolved that anonymity which characterizes the Roman, the Alpine and the Quaker.

The circumstances of this kind of life, though
fostering the qualities referred to, are nevertheless not
ultimate enough to account for their origin, and here
we have to go back to racial foundations and the dis-
tinguishing feature of the short round head.   The
long-head is the natural and instinctive head, and a
great change in character supervened with its modification, if indeed it ever became modified.   The
Mediterranean with his quick response to stimulus,
the Nordic with his love of combat and rule are but
Nature's children, playing with toys.   They all have
the characteristics and the weaknesses of our *unconscious*—childish vanity and egotism ; while at first
they responded naturally, as they grew and met with
opposition they were inclined, like the individual, to
become the prey of infantile complexes.   Louis XIV
or Napoleon with their soldiers and their conquests,
lauded of the Nordics, are yet foolish children to the
philosopher.   They had worked out no philosophy of

life, they did not realize their fellow-man, they can hardly be said to have developed a soul.

Head-shape gave the Alpine a better brain which compensated for defects in his sensory powers. His light was turned inwards and he developed that idealism which served as a secondary environment. Acquiring and classifying knowledge he fostered this inner environment and, if it be true that a man merely responds to stimuli, he was able to respond to a world which was far wider, deeper and older than the mere external. Our great heritage of memory, scholarship, philosophy and finally morality is largely due to this short-headed influence. If a man responds merely to external environment he is merely non-moral, Undine without her soul; if he responds to the environment within him he has developed something of a soul and is on the way to morality. The first sees men and things, but does not realize them, just as a savage sees a steamship but does not realize it; but the new brain led men to realize things and men, made other men's joys and sufferings their own, and, finally, gave them a soul. That learning and idealism may be and have been abused is too well known, but it is probably right in the end that knowledge and morality are synonymous and that idealism is man's greatest step to a higher plane.

CHAPTER V

THE MEDITERRANEAN

Our population to-day exhibits the peculiar feature that whereas its culture is strongly Nordic, its somatic characters, particularly its head-shape, are mainly Mediterranean, so that we are in a large measure what Mr H. G. Wells has called pseudomorphs. The reason for this is that the long-head is the more natural head, being of great antiquity, and there is a constant tendency for it to wipe out its more artificial rival. The long narrow head is not only more easily perpetuated owing to the physical conditions of birth, but it must be remembered that the oldest stocks in the country, particularly women, are Mediterranean and Hamitic, and not only is heredity weighted in favour of the dolichocephals, but the centrifugal force of woman in race-moulding is also on their side. Sexual selection has also doubtless helped, and the man who has always appealed most to women has been the Nordic who, despite his modifications, is but a glorified Mediterranean. His tall stature, blond colouring, his strength, athleticism and commanding nature, are all calculated to appeal to women, as is evidenced by Ouida's novels, in contrast to the round-faced, plodding, serious Alpine or the untidy, badly-dressed, beetle-browed Beaker-man.

The Mediterranean is essentially a town-dweller, and forms to-day the bulk of the population of our large cities; owing to his somewhat thriftless and undependable character he is found among the lower and submerged classes from which he tends to drift into the Navy or the town regiments of the Army. The servant class is largely recruited from this stock, also artisans and many of no, or doubtful, occupation.

He is short of stature, with dark hair and eyes, long and thin of face and wiry of build. His eyes and face are sharp, and the street urchin with his ready quip, his ability to seize or make an opportunity, is characteristic of the race.

Never distinguised for truth, morality or altruism, this type lives for itself and for the moment, but possesses nevertheless qualities which are valuable in the racial-make up. Its ready wit, imagination, sensitiveness become an asset in the artistic and literary world, and we have only to compare English literature with German, or English life with Swiss to observe the difference imparted by this racial admixture. The Mediterranean is naturalistic and a vehicle of the *unconscious*, possibly of a general and ultimate unconscious and, less dominated by the conscious censor, he is capable of genius; moreover, unamenable to routine, he is an experimenter both for good and evil, and the race benefits both by his successes and his failures. It is his temperament which inspires "Bohemia," introducing long hair and extravagant manners.

His catabolism is a wonderful antidote to the anabolic Alpine or the conventional Nordic, for his sharp wit penetrates below the surface of respectability and artificiality.   His values are not pecuniary, and he is able to appreciate the realities of life and its sensuous beauties.   If he loves wine, women and extravagance, he can also appreciate colour, natural beauty and the exquisiteness of poetry and the arts.

The Mediterranean, in sharp contrast to the Alpine, is a natural gambler, and it is significant that as we are becoming enfranchized from Scottish and Puritan dominance, there is a tendency to legalize betting.

In industry the Mediterranean does not shine except in one direction, and that is engineering.   I do not mean large constructional work in which a considerable amount of planning, mathematical calculation and general architectonics are required, nor the plodding routine of the marine engineer, for in both these the Scot holds the field except where Englishmen of kindred psychology are able to push their way in sporadically.   But it is in the lighter branches of engineering, electrical and motor-car work, that the Mediterranean is at home, and the modern garage staff is composed almost entirely of men of this race, their essentially Mediterranean weaknesses being well known to those who employ them.   It is interesting in connection with this type of engineering to compare the important part played by the Italians and the French, for the dashing nature and the mechanical skill of the Mediterranean find free play in this direction.   While the French excel in finished workmanship, they are, on the whole, more solid engineers than the Italians.   But in electrical and motor engineering the Italian shows his peculiar aptitude, and he is able to penetrate into our own great electrical enterprises, where the names Marconi, Pirelli and Ferranti are household words.

According to some American standards the engineer stands first in the scale of efficiency and, in the American view, of intelligence. It is quite comprehensible that, subjected to numerous tests on an efficiency machine, the engineer of the Mediterranean type could show very good results, for his strong point is ready reaction to stimulus, but to ascribe this to intellectual power is the reverse of correct, for the intellectual man is one who by dint of his freedom of choice responds slowly to stimulus. Schopenhauer said that the characteristics of the German was dull-wittedness ; we may in some degree say the same of the Scot ; but this is in virtue of his superfluity of intellect, not of his lack of it. Quickness in repartee was the perquisite of the old 'bus-driver and is still noticeable in the London streets, while both the Scot and the philosopher are slow in the uptake. The strength of these engineers is that they see a machine and its working intuitively ; they can look at an engine and know its functions almost without examination. It is a matter of pure intuition ; they are functions of environment. And as to invention, this seldom comes to the student, but is an inspiration of the unconscious in which the Mediterranean is so strong. But ask these men to write a constructive report, and it will probably be random and illogical ; get them to talk on general subjects and they will pour out all the latest balderdash from some rag of a newspaper.

In this connection the vogue of wireless among the lower middle classes is of great interest. The clerk, the shop-assistant, the hairdresser have now become not only listeners but experts. They not only understand wireless sets, but can make them. This is of very great importance, since a knowledge of electricity is a knowledge of one of the deepest and most final of nature's secrets, and it becomes a question whether the make-up of a man with a good knowledge of electricity is not superior to that of the philosopher who can understand *Appearance and Reality*. It may be that here we have an instance of nature coming into her own; philosophy has for centuries abused by excess the gift of intellect; in its application to life and the facts of life it displays its real uses and ends, and in this way, by combining some learning with innate cleverness, the Mediterranean may be pushing on to ultimate victory.

CHAPTER VI

RELIGION AND MORALITY

THE position of the Nordic in relation to Christianity is somewhat anomalous, and a people with less egotistic idealism might feel cramped by its conditions. It is possible however that in connection with the theory of empire the climax may arise and have to be faced, if such is not the case already.   In the past the Englishman, never failing to bring everything to the touchstone of conscience, has been able to satisfy himself with the conclusion that his rule has been in the interests of the ruled and, if his subjects did not see this, it was owing to their barbaric lack of intelligence.   With the growth of sympathy and the objective point of view, and possibly with the dilution of the purely Nordic idea with other ethnic currents of a Shavian nature, a spirit of self-criticism has grown up which makes for the health of the community but may be fatal to imperialistic foundations. We are already on the horns of a dilemma : if we treat a subject native race on purely Biblical and Christian lines our Empire cannot last a day ; if, on the other hand, we continue to treat them Nordically, we are no longer Christians.   It is only by a series of fictions that a Christian empire is carried on and, as soon as we are honest enough to question those fictions, the

position becomes critical. Historically speaking it
was only by a fiction that the greater part of the
Nordic race accepted Christianity at all ; and it has
been maintained by a continuation of these fictions
which the migratory ego of the race is so eminently
fitted for maintaining. It is due to a most elaborate
fiction that the squire has sat for centuries of Sundays
under the parson and heard that the only way of
salvation is to sell all he has and give to the poor, or
that the path of the rich man to heaven is as difficult
as it is for a camel to pass through a needle's eye.
The fiction is that the doctrine does not apply to
squires or that it is a kind of parable with a heavenly
meaning and not intended literally ; and to this
fiction every well-bred person subscribes. But there
is absolutely no evidence that Christ did not mean
what He said. The fact is that the Nordic is not a
Christian but a ruler ; he holds practically none of
the tenets of Christianity. Yet he finds the Church
useful for many reasons ; it bolsters up his class, his
rule and his traditions ; on the other hand it both
contents the people and keeps them in subjection.
But for its extreme usefulness Christianity would
never have been adopted and perpetuated by the
Nordics ; utterly alien to their own spirit it has been
constantly used to fortify their rule. It has been said
that its first acceptance among the Jews was due to
the fact that in a time of hopelessness and bitter
persecution it offered the only possible consolation—
happiness and glory in a future life ; hence its great
appeal to the poor and suffering. It is not the religion
of the eugenist but of the dysgenist ; the poorer, more

miserable, more suffering a person was, the greater his future reward. The Nordic has accepted and supported it because it not only made his subjects content with their burdens but actually encouraged them to seek greater suffering. The Nordic is essentially eugenic and, in the same measure, unchristian. Quite apart from the purely religious aspect of the mission and teachings of Jesus Christ which is not dealt with here, the question must ultimately arise, when we are honest enough to face it, which is to survive, the Nordic spirit or the Christian ? The former is one of the principle mainstays of civilization ; with the loss of empire follows anarchy, possibly the end of a great race. Christianity, on the other hand, has an individual value and significance, and possibly the only satisfactory conclusion can be reached when the aims of the community and the individual are one ; that is when the individual is social and unselfish enough to dispense with sovereignty.

The time is full of dilemma and it is possible for the spirit of morality to conflict seriously with life itself. Many vegetarians, for instance, are actuated by the conviction that it is morally wrong to take the life of their fellow creatures, yet their tenets appear to some to cause serious bodily deterioration. The problem is similar to that of empire, the withdrawal of which might lead to bloodshed, crime and destruction. We seem to require a philosophy of life which accepts a certain amount of evil and cruelty in order to maintain a balance of good, and it is desirable that something of the kind be evolved before the conflict of opinion leads to chaos. At present we do not recognize the evil so long as it suits our purpose to ignore it—another Nordic fiction.

There is a further aspect in which it is difficult to reconcile the Nordic spirit with Christianity, or even with religion at all. In late years religion has taken on a new psychological aspect ; it is one of the great sublimations of the thwarted wish ; in particular it is the sublimation of the Œdipus complex, the hyper-trophied love of the mother. Religion with the Mediterranean fits very well into the psychological frame, for the true Catholic spirit is one of resignation, as if life were too much for the earthly sufferer, who needs to feel that the everlasting arms are beneath him ; it was the spirit of the Greeks, in that they felt Necessity too great for suffering mortals, and found a sublimation in the drama. But the Nordic is not like this. He has no Œdipus complex and, as to fate, the Nordic English boy has been compared to Aladdin, the favourite of fortune, especially if he passes through Eton and Balliol. I have said else-where that the difference between the Protestant and the Catholic is that one is above God and the other below Him, and, although there is a differance between the Nordic and the Alpine Protestant, we feel that neither adopts a servile attitude. The Hebrews spoke much of fearing God, and so does the Koran, but what exactly is this fear ? The Jews insisted on a fair bargain, a covenant ; the Scotch have since done the same ; the Almighty must do as He is done by, and must expect no better treatment than He gives. That is the Old Testament spirit. I strongly suspect that into the fear of God there enters another element, for the people I remember as talking most about it were very fearsome old gentlemen themselves. The terrible God which our progenitors set up for us to worship is in no small degree a replica of themselves, as Jehovah was of the patriarchal chief. The fear that was inculcated is the fear that the paterfamilias demanded from his women and children ; so it is with the dissenting Alpine, the John Knox type. God and religion to the Nordic are a useful form representing order, stability, and proper hierarchy ; God and the King whom they outwardly honour are inwardly the mainstay and support of their class.

Mr H. G. Wells once referred to our love for the imagery of the sun-dry Levant, constituting so large a part of the Bible. Surely in future years it will be a matter of wonder how the religion and folk-lore of desert Palestine entered into the hearts and lives of the people of cold, foggy *ultima Thule*. The racial and psychological reasons are a matter for speculation. The Bible, of course, is the foundation of Christianity, but that is hardly a reason why it should mean so much to the people of Britain. The original Christian tradition is found in the Roman Church, and to the Romanists the Bible is little known and means less. In Ireland there is a tendency to treat archangels and Biblical personages in the " hail fellow well met " spirit so characteristic of the national temperament and tradition. Bible worship is then clearly not Mediterranean. If we consider its geographical distribution and the character of its exponents we may get some sort of racial clue to the tradition. Bible-cult is found in Scotland, particularly the Lowlands, the Midlands, East Anglia, Wales, Cornwall and Tunbridge Wells, all tinctured with a brachycephalic admixture. Apart from Cornwall and Wales we note the presence of Beaker, Alpine and Anglian blood; in Cornwall and Wales we have the remnants of the Brythons combined with a Mongoloid strain. In regard to persons we think of Wycliffe and Wesley; Bunyan, Milton and Cromwell; More, Colet and Erasmus; Wycliffe connects with Hus, the Hungarian, and Asiatic brachycephaly; the Lollards are named from *lollen*, to sing, and remind us both of the Welsh and the *Meistersänger*—to sing in chorus is brachycephalic; the dolichocephals, being individual and not having the co-ordination for team work, bear the soloist tradition. More, Colet and Erasmus represent the Renaissance which has not yet, I think, been associated with anything racial, but in Colet's enthusiasm and his desire that the ploughman and the peasant woman should be able to know and take comfort in the actual words of the Bible we have something which is essentially anti-Catholic, which partakes of the spirit of Luther whose desire was to abolish intermediaries and go straight to God. The dolicephal is the materialist, the brachycephal the idealist; it is the brachycephal who leads the way to abstraction and to the single abstract deity.

Bunyan and Cromwell are actual short-heads and their party was known as the " Roundheads," the Eastern counties where they originated being the stronghold of the Beaker-folk, reinforced later, by Alpines and Angles; the same mixture of blood is found in the Lowlands of Scotland where the Round-heads discovered sure and like-thinking allies.

The descendants of the Roundheads are the Dissenters and if the Roundheads were, as I believe, racial round-heads or brachycephals, the Dissenters are what they are owing to their brachycephaly. Their devotion to the Bible, the Word, is well known,

As there is no ethnical reason why people of Alpine and Asiatic stock should find an essential interest in the religion of Palestine and its neighbourhood we must look for the cause in some other direction, and it is probably found in the nature of the teaching of the Bible, particularly of the New Testament. Mr H. G. Wells in his *Outline of History* has drawn attention to the ancient feud between priest and prophet, and it is on the prophetic side that the Bible, particularly the New Testament, makes its appeal. And herein may lie the reason of its less intimate appeal to the Roman Church and the ritualists generally. Christ and the prophets were rebels against priest-craft which is wrapped up with the magical traditions of the tribe ; they stood for independence and for direct approach to God ; for a moral personal life. The diatribes of the prophets against idols, images, and local deities, so familiar even in these days to those who have sojourned around the Mediterranean, are repeated in Milton's or John Knox's scourgings of the Scarlet Woman.

Mr Peake suggests that the Alpine represents the Quaker type, and indeed there was much in the life of these communal lake-dwellers which gave promise of the strong characters which mark not only the

Quakers, but the New England settlers, and the Puritans generally. The nature of their settlements, wherein each depended on the other, tolerated no superior class and no nobility save that of sacrifice and labour, and here perhaps may be found the reason for that contrast once made between Rome and Athens, that the Roman tree ran all to wood, whereas Athens was a bower of leaves. According to latest researches Rome seems to have been founded by a *terramara* or Alpine folk, and her early history is full of heroes like Cincinnatus who exchanged the ploughshare for generalship. In course of time the differences between Roman and subject people became emphasized, and the Romans themselves became a dominant class. But among themselves it was considered a bad thing for one man to set himself above others or to differentiate himself in any way ; their genius, contrary to the Athenian, has been called anonymous. And we remember that right to the end of the republic this feeling persisted ; Cicero's speeches are full of it, and it was Julius Cæsar's supposed ambition and his designs upon a throne which led to his death. This hatred of kingship as an institution is well known to us in our own country, its greatest manifestation being presented in the Roundhead revolution, which was in fact an Alpine revolt. Since the restoration a stigma has attached to those who are not in favour of kingship, and it has been customary to charge them with disloyalty and petty jealousy. We must not forget however that they are of the same stock as Cincinnatus and Brutus. The hatred of kingship and aristocracy is an echo of the communal life of Rome, and of the Swiss Cantons ; Brutus and William Tell were both Alpines.

The Quaker is a type of extraordinary distinction, having many racial traits. The tall stature, clean features and square jaw are typically Alpine. The anonymity in the Quakers' religion, in their charity and even in their dress is an important feature of the brachycephalic type. In business the Quaker lays brick upon brick and adds pound to pound, avoiding speculation and relying upon thrift. Whereas the Jew deals in goods which admit of an element of doubt and uncertainty alike as to quality, size and character, such as diamonds, greengrocery, clothes and glass, the Quaker usually confines himself to the staples of life, particularly food, actuated possibly to some extent by the steadiness of the demand, but more especially from his ancient agricultural traditions and his communal activities. In character he is self-effacing, using as few words as possible, but he is noted for steady, useful and beneficial action. In his religious services he tolerates no priest ; all are equal in the sight of God ; and one may only rise above the others if moved by the spirit and illuminated by the Inner Light. The Light of the Mediterraneans is external, that of the Quakers internal, and in the latter folk we find particularly that abstraction which was the gift to the world of the short-headed peoples. Their attitude towards externals is an eminent mark of distinction between short-heads and long, between the ultimate Asiatic and the ultimate Hamite, and it is typified in the contrast between the barn-like appearance of the Presbyterian Church and the ornate cathedral of the Catholics. The inner significance of this difference may perhaps be found in the tenets of the Behaviourist theory of psychology, that man's behaviour is a function of environment ; he merely re-acts ; but the environment may be extended by knowledge far beyond the scope of the physical, so that a man may react finally not to his physical surroundings, but to the ideal content of his mind. And it is the creation of this ideal content, which may in a sense be regarded as the Inner Light, that the brachycephals excelled. In this connection it may be noted that the idealists of Europe have always been the Germans, who are notable for their brachycephalic element. It is also interesting to consider that the character of the Quaker is closely resembled by that of the Lowland Scot, who is also permeated in some degree by brachycephaly.

While not competing with the Germans, Swiss, Scotch and New England Americans, the English are a moral nation in the narrower sense of the term. Of late years we have been shocked by crimes of violence, but these belong largely to the Mediterranean stratum of the population, who naturally tend to increase faster than any other. The growing tendency to divorce, while it may be condemned by the hypercritical, represents a healthy tendency towards adjustment to changing conditions. The old marriage, based on the capture and enslavement of women, could only endure while the subjection of women lasted. As morality grows, the foundations of marriage totter like those of empire, and the breaking of the marital bonds when love ceases is in the interests of a higher morality. Moreover both as regards crime and divorce, the incident of the Great War has been a disturbing factor.

But the English norm of morality is slow to alter, and it is best evidenced in a London chop-house or the commercial-room of an hotel. Though the men you meet there will be free in their jokes, and may be superficially loose, they have yet at bottom a very rigid and uniform code covering various items ; that a man must pay his debts and keep his word, that he must treat his wife well, but keep her in control ; that he must work or be employed for so many hours a day ; that at all costs he personally must be properly fed and clothed ; in addition to a few simple tenets of this kind he has certain abhorrences, as of night-clubs, dancing, marital laxness, the Catholic Church, high-brows, the Jews, Bernard Shaw and the *Daily News* ; on the other hand he owes a certain, though not rabid, allegiance to Protestantism, the King and Constitution and various national institutions.

Nordic morality has already been dealt with. While not varying materially in tone from the last, it differs in outlook, being perhaps somewhat more interested and less sincere, for it is the code of a dominant race which must perforce maintain its position. Thus its support of King, Constitution and Church is in large part a matter of self-support. The Nordic keeps his word and is a man of honour, but these things have a conventional interpretation. The great sin to him is the sin against good form. In fact you can do anything so long as you observe the rules.

The Mediterraneans were never distinguished for morality and they may be left out at this stage. But lest these observations appear to give an unfair representation of our people, I must hasten to say that in morality as in most other things we embrace both extremes, the best and the worst. And if morality is interpreted in its highest and most transcendental sense, we shall find that many English people rise to great heights. The influence of the broad-head with its idealism has led to the birth of a conscience and perhaps of a soul. But it seems that a soul may be born in two ways, either of knowledge or of intuition. With Vaughan and the mystics the realization of others and sympathy with them is of the latter kind ; nor does it stop at humanity, but seems to embrace God, Nature and the Universe. It is by such paths that the Mediterraneans rise to the heights of virtue and morality, and in the Catholic Church to mystic ecstasies. The morality of the Protestant and of the Englishman is of a different character, being based more on reason, knowledge and utility. Thus it may be discriminating and uncharitable, giving only to worthy causes, and tempering mercy with justice. It is often a hard kind of virtue based upon conscience and, carried to its extreme, becomes the Non-conformist Conscience, bequeathed to us by the Puritans and Alpines.

Thus while our virtue is on a lofty human scale it seldom touches the divine, and though we have our Florence Nightingales we have no Jeanne Darc.

CHAPTER VII

INTELLECT AND EDUCATION

ALTHOUGH England has possessed and still possesses learned men, learning is not a strong point of our prevailing culture as it is with the Scotch or the Germans. From the comparison it may be gathered that it is rather to be associated with the brachycephals, and this is indeed the case. The short-head harks back to Asia whence comes the love of learning for itself alone. The Mongols, an extreme type of the brachycephals, plunderers and murderers as they were, regarded learned men with something akin to reverence. With short-headed man appears to have developed a hypertrophy of the brain-lobes at the expense of both the senses and intuition, and from the example of China we see how learning becomes, instead of a means to an end, an end in itself. There is a touching picture in Lady Hosie's *Two Gentlemen of China* of one of her amiable hosts who reached a climax in his career of examinations by being admitted to the Forest of Pencils so that it became difficult to assign him a government post commensurate with his academic distinction, and in reading this I could not help recalling a similar case in England rather over twenty years ago when a gentleman passed so high in the Civil Service Examination, obtaining nearly full marks in several subjects, that he had to be kept waiting until a suitable post could be found for him. It should be noted that neither gentleman had shown or had any opportunity of showing any capacity for the work of government, although both were doubtless capable officials. The peculiarity of both systems is that the examination has no relation to official requirements, just as much of our learning has no relation to life. It is common knowledge that men of exceptional efficiency in the Civil Service have had to be turned out because they could not pass theoretical examinations, and quite rightly according to the rules of the service. But it seems somewhat anomalous that a poor official should be preferred to a good one simply because he is adept at something wholly different from the work he is expected to do. This marvellous system in England is largely due to Lord Macaulay, himself a Whig, and therefore carrying on the brachycephalic tradition. The Nordics have no hand in it, for they despise both learning and the Civil Service. They go to school for sports and then pass into the Army or other gentlemanly occupations. The Nordic type is not found in the Civil Service, whose higher ranks are peopled generally by small men with large heads and of no particular race. Ethnically they are transcendentalists, vulgarly known at school as " swots " and at college eschewing games. I do not think they are any worse for this, and indeed they probably represent the most intellectual, conscientious and independent type in a country where these qualities show distinct signs of decay.

An important aspect of the case, however, is the

lack of co-ordination of means to an end, a failing characteristic of our administrative and governmental activities and even in some degree of our commerce. For it has long been a reproach to our business methods that we produce what we think people ought to have instead of what they want. When I lived in South Africa it was the custom to buy a cooking-stove for one's house, and one was always faced with the alternative of an expensive English stove, which was not quite suitable but would last for ever, and the cheap foreign stove, which would last only the few years required of it but was eminently fitted for its purpose. Herein is seen the *a priori* nature of English methods. Deduction means reasoning from principles and induction reasoning from facts ; the first starts with the mind and the ego and is Asiatic ; the second with the external world and is intuitive and Mediterranean. The difference is traceable to head-shape and leads us to contrast the orthocephalic and the heterocephalic. It seems probable that the long-head of the Mediterranean is the right and natural head, whereas the squarer head of the Asiatics is in the nature of an experiment. There are several arguments to be adduced in support of this conclusion. The long-head is very ancient and in this country goes back to the river-bed gravels, whereas in Africa it is of the remotest antiquity. It has been found that as regards the chances of life nature favours the dolichocephal ; the head is an important factor in birth and the long, narrow head has advantages in this respect. Those who have read that important psychological study, *Lummox*, will remember the old charwoman's ecstasy over the head-shape of one of her many mistresses, and how it reminded her of an egg slipping out of the mouth; the ovoid is one of the most important of the Mediterranean cranial shapes. Again, it is to be noticed that in the British Isles the long-head has almost eclipsed the other so that despite the prevalence of Nordic and Asiatic culture the short-head itself is scarcely ever found; and in Ireland it has always been a noticeable phenomenon that the Irishry tended to swallow up any stragglers outside the Pale. The view is confirmed by a consideration of the comparative attitudes of the two peoples towards life: the Greeks, full of the Mediterranean naturalism and *joie de vivre*, seem essentially the people who made the most of life and were most in accord with it and, as life is perhaps the most real part of our existence, one's use and enjoyment of it must necessarily be a test of the rightness of one's outlook; if on the other hand we turn to one of our dour Bible-students of the Midlands or Southern Scotland we cannot help feeling that, brought to the touchstone of life, they are a failure. For one thing they admit this themselves in that they belittle this life with a view to a problematic one in the future; the Puritan, whose spirit is by no means dead, mortified the senses, denying himself the enjoyment of form and colour, of good food, music, and in fact all the benefits of reality. The Greeks worshipped the body, our Asiatics in their interpretation of Christian principles mortified it. The Greeks were endowed with very good eyes, and were distinguished by sight and perception; the Asiatics had poor eyes and turned away from the outer to the inner light. This matter of the eye is a very important one racially, and those who compare the shape of the eye-sockets of the two kinds of skulls will observe how in the short skull the socket has been squared and the line of the sockets drawn up from a curve towards a straight line. This distinction seems to have affected the vision, and it is a noticeable fact that the wearing of spectacles is very common among brachycephalic peoples like the Germans. Goethe, who had a strain of both races in him, has been condemned as a philosopher by his own people because he saw too well, and the Greeks have been criticized in the same way and for the same reasons by the more Asiatic and idealist philosophers. I cannot help thinking of a typical Mediterranean of my acquaintance who excels in most sports, and does so naturally; to see him play billiards is a revelation to the student of ethnology; there is no thinking or calculating, but his behaviour at the table is just a function of his environment and he responds naturally and accurately. Dancing again is another racial test; the Mediterranean dances naturally, the Asiatic tries to dance logically and mathematically. And finally, to conclude this discussion on the comparative attitudes to life we might contrast the educational schemes of Froebel and Montessori, the first always harping on aim and theory, the second realistic, sensuous and imbued with the worship of life and with the desire of making its pupils fit into its scheme.

These arguments will perhaps assist in explaining that divorce between means and end which characterizes so much of our administrative work. And there is moreover another influence ascribable to the Puritan and Asiatic tradition, the love of work in itself. I once heard an American story of a young manager who was given the chance of reorganizing a business which had proved too great a burden for his predecessor. After a few days some of the directors entered his office to see how he was progressing and found him sitting with his feet on the mantel-piece, doing nothing. With laudable insight they immediately doubled his salary, recognizing the genius which could do the job with the minimum of effort. In this country his salary would have been reduced or he would have been discharged. Economically labour is the disutility at the cost of which utility is produced. In the popular English mind however labour is something laudable and moral. The man who works early and late is praised, whereas those who have an insight into his office may know that he is actually creating work, making life a burden to his colleagues, and clogging the wheels of the machine ; they may know that the work actually goes better in his absence, so that he is really a minus quantity. But usually such men are applauded according to the hours they work, the actual output being disregarded. If anyone does the work in a quarter of the time, he is regarded as superficial, a flash in the pan. Women will ask a man how many hours he works, as if he were a machine, and sneer if he returns home early ; and yet in an hour he may have done what others could not have done in a year.

There are men naturally fitted to certain jobs and

therefore they do them easily and without effort. That they do so is part of their genius, and this is a thing which the English are unable to understand. If work in an office goes wrong and gets behindhand, they put more men into it, and the work goes wronger and gets further behind. What is required is as few as possible of the right men ; any additions are encumbrances. But this incorrect point of view has actuated many schemes which have been otherwise laudable ; as of placing ex-service men in government offices, replacing others who may not have the same moral claims, but who could actually do the work. Because a man has fought for his country and become wounded it does not follow that he is suitable to any particular job, and the result is that the job is done not by a suitable man, but by any man, who may or may not be suitable. The idea, partaking both of the Scotch and Puritan spirit, is one of *perfectabilité*, and assumes that, given certain moral qualifications, one man is as good as another and moreover that, the higher his moral standard in respect of drink, women, dancing and the like, the better fitted he is for any particular job. Yet real genius is a breaking through the cap of the conscious, so that the unconscious wells through, and this accounts for the fact that most men of genius have exhibited in some way a slight declension from the normal or moral standard.

A man may be a journalist or a grocer and may be good or bad at his trade, because every calling demands a certain aptitude or genius. The Puritan and general English view is that a man goes to work and does so many hours' journalism or butchering, which is, of course, absurd. The great inspiration of one's life might come, as with Coleridge, in one's sleep.

It is to be hoped that the theory of Relativity as expounded by Professor Eddington may assist in a saner view of a man and his job. The theory of relativity may be regarded in a sense as a theory of the natural track in time-space. Every man, like every object, has his natural track. Our educational tendency is to get a man off in the wrong track, and he may or may not find the right one. *If Winter Comes* tells the story of the man who was on the wrong track and only ultimately found the right one.

But beyond the fact that one man is regarded as potentially equal to another in all respects, there is another Puritan one that work, being naturally unpleasant, is therefore in itself a moral good. My father used to tell a story, with what foundation I know not, of a boy, I believe Sir Walter Scott, who coming into dinner on a cold day remarked how fine the soup was. Hs father said to the servant : " Put some water in that boy's soup." That is the Puritan attitude towards work.

My own experience leads me to this conclusion, that if a man in an office were set to prove that two and two equal four, he might proceed in two ways. Usually, knowing the ropes, he would put in a considerable amount of overtime, fill sheets of paper and, if the result came out that two and two equalled five, he would earn approbation and promotion, provided he had written enough. If he proved in a few words that two and two equalled four and then went home, he would be written down a slacker.

And here another factor enters into the case, namely the love of words, not vain words, but weighty and argumentative words, whether they be in a Presbyterian sermon, an article in the *Observer*, or an official minute. What they mean, what is the conclusion, is immaterial, so that many and high-sounding words be there. The predilection of the Scotch for these exercises, taken in conjunction with German philosophy and the Roman forum, as contrasted with the economy and lucidity of the French or the Greeks, their sure and direct adaptation of means to end, proclaim the tradition to be Asiatic, a phenomenon of the hypertrophied intellect as opposed to a direct sensing of actuality.

My father, who was a great student of the Bible, used to be very scornful of the Jews' attitude towards work as exemplified in the expulsion of Adam from the Garden and the curse of labour put upon him. He used to say that work was man's greatest blessing, and so in a way it is. On the other hand, that it should be a blessing may not altogether be a good thing, for recent psychological developments tend to show that it is, like religion, one of the great sublimations, namely, an escape from life, and that is what our great workers find it. They fill up their time with work, and work till their dying day for the reason that they are unable to live. It is all part of that escape from life, from the senses, from actuality, which characterizes our education and our general conduct, our heritage from the idealists of Asia who could not see, and turned their vision inwards to obtain compensation for the loss of the real world. Men work so hard because they go mad if they don't; because they are unable to take leisure. With part of our population it has become a disease, though the Nordic has happily kept free from it; he always maintained the tradition of the happy savage who made others work for him, and devoted himself to hunting and fighting as he now does to sport. The rest have worked for him so long that they have come to regard their slavery as a privilege and, whereas the Nordic has always enjoyed the benefit of unemployment, they regard it with horror. He is a wise and happy man indeed who can enjoy and appreciate leisure. Those of our workers who retain something of the old Adam do indeed show some appreciation of it while paying lip-service to work or at least employment.

In a country like England was before the war, a country whose income greatly exceeded her expenditure, a considerable amount of leisure and unemployment was an economic result. It is a popular fallacy that a rich country means one in which everyone is working. In the perfectly rich country there would be perfect idleness. Our population therefore, in its industrial efforts, is working to an end it neither understands nor appreciates. With a better distribution of wealth, unemployment is more equally shared, falls more largely upon the poorer classes and, as we tend to get richer and juster, the tendency will be more and more in this direction. The excess of income, if and when it increases, will tend more and more with our growing morality to be distributed among the poorer section of the community, so that an increase of wealth will necessarily mean an increase of doles or their equivalent. Our population seems hardly ripe for this, and regards the dole as an evil. In present circumstances it is, but we have to face a prospect of its being permanent. Our upper classes have always had doles, and in their case there has been no great outcry against the evil. Why should they be an evil when given to Tom, Dick and Harry? If these men can learn to use their dole as the Nordics did, all should be well, and in any case we have got to frame our politics to meet such conditions.

Our culture is said to be Nordic. Yet in certain respects our institutions, though supported by the Nordics, seem alien to their nature. Our religion is one, our education another, and both are based on the principle of an escape from life. It is probably because they were once one and the same thing, our schools and universities being based largely upon religious foundations. Moreover in our education two streams unite, the clerico-religious and the meta-physico-Asiatic, both despising life, one for its vanities, the other because of its sensuousness. In the first aspect our education has not freed itself from the methods of the Schoolmen, and there is still a tendency to specialize in two dead languages to the exclusion of all else, and to treat even them as laboratory specimens. Each branch of learning is regarded as being in a water-tight compartment and we require so much history, so much Latin, so much mathematics, as if we were buying groceries, although I admit that there is a growing tendency to broaden the educational outlook. The tradition, however, is to treat every subject as if it were isolated, bottled and dead and, just as our clergy of all denominations turn ever and ever the same square yard of earth, telling us always the same thing in new or the same words, so in education the tendency has always been to go deeper and deeper instead of wider and wider, so that the man in the street is now better informed than the man in the study. Most humble clerks now have a wireless set, many can make them, and not a few thoroughly understand them, and this fact leads to considerable scientific and really useful knowledge. Your philosopher has speculated for centuries on the nature of matter or of space, but in electricity you have the origin of matter and probably the origin of space, since space seems to be a function of matter. The philosopher dwells in the regions of abstract thought, his pride being that his reasoning has no relation to actuality or utility. He is satisfied with himself, but the world, not satisfied with him, is passing him by, for the ultimate and the absolute will not be found in his study nor in his brain, but in the physical laboratory and in real life. Pure mathematics were supposed to be similarly divorced from actuality, but some of their equations were recently found to be equivalent to the laws of time-space and led to the theory of Relativity and the Quantum Theory, the latter of which appears to approach some sort of finality. In the hypertrophy of the brain and the ego we seem to have been wasting our time and, whereas our savants express regret that our moneyed classes now no longer speak the King's English, they are really condemning themselves, for if life is a fact, the good life is a desideratum, and money is a necessary preliminary. It seems to me that the prosperous are those who best fit into their environment and it is they who are the most successful livers. I know of no better standard than life itself. And if prosperity and education have become divorced it is surely education which is wrong. The Asiatics taught us to escape from life, and it is the Mediterranean spirit which is going to bring us back. The Montessori system for instance is founded on a worship of life and aims at an accommodation to life.

The Nordic uses the public schools and the universities for sport, not for education. The public school produces a type, or perhaps two types, the same in manner and speech, but the one a scholar, the other not. The scholar generally passes on to the university. But in the end both types are alike in that they have passed through the uniform mould which has no relation to any future purpose, and they have to make what they can of life without any preparation for it. Those succeed best who soonest forget their education. In the sheltered professions, the Army, Navy, Church, the Civil Service and to a limited extent the Law, the standards are the Nordic and public school standards, so that the most Nordic and least individual will often succeed. But commerce and industry are striding ahead of the professions and are more and more setting the standards of wealth and of life, and here the public school and 'Varsity men are outside their element and can only make good by shaking off their traditions.

It is part of our educational theory to avoid

specialization, especially in the early stages, the aim being to train the mind without warping it in one direction and to build up something in the nature of a soul. There is a great deal in this point of view but it is open to certain criticisms. In our higher education at least this lack of specialization is apt to continue to the end and the young man enters life entirely untrained. And whereas it is perhaps difficult to ascertain a child's true bent in early years, it may be urged on the other hand that he never has an opportunity of disclosing it. Most people have a genius in some particular direction ; not only are they not in general given an opportunity of displaying and pursuing this, but too often it is crushed out altogether by the uniform curriculum. In this way there is a tremendous loss of progress and efficiency, even of beauty and happiness in the world. In the Montessori system the Mediterranean love of the real and the sensuous is exemplified ; the children are surrounded by objects and material, and respond naturally to them. They are not taught. It is simple reaction to environment, but it is a wide and diversified environment, so that it gives a child an opportunity of responding in the manner most suitable to it. I am inclined to think that this system should be extended throughout our educational system, so that at the school and university there should be opportunities of engaging in any of life's pursuits ; education should be life in little, where individual experiments could be carried out without danger. The Germans, although as a rule the most confirmed idealists, had yet a point or two in their educational system which have met with general commendation. One is their *Abiturient* certificate which records the pupil's character and aptitudes during education, his *dossier* in fact, which if based upon an elastic system such as I have touched upon, would be extremely useful in placing a boy in after life, in preference to the results of examinations in purely theoretical subjects.   Another is the *Wanderjahr* in which the youth makes his travel-tour, becoming acquainted with the needs and practices of actual life before entering upon it.

If English intellect is not of the first order, neither perhaps was the Greek ; the Germans at least would class neither very highly.   It must be remembered however that a powerful intellect necessarily connotes neither common sense nor a special fitness for life, but rather the reverse.   The Englishman, standing midway between the Scot who has too much intellect and the Irishman who has too little, has the advantages which are found in the middle path.

One of the disadvantages of the intellect is that it obscures the intuitive power and genius, so that inspiration finds it difficult to break through the cap of the conscious.   Thus new ideas and inventions are not discovered by men of intellect but by men of intuition.   In intellect as in other things the English display a wide range, for they possess in a marked degree the characteristics of the races which go to their making, the intellectual Beaker-man, the practical and logical Alpine, the emotional Mediterranean, and the intellectually hide-bound and stable Nordic.   As however it is the Nordic culture which prevails with us, we generally affect a careless stupidity which may disguise deep thought or keenness; the Englishman is seldom such a fool as he allows himself to appear.

By the virtue of Nordic dominance his views are conservative and tradition weighs very heavily with him. His laws broaden down from precedent to precedent and are painfully slow in doing so. Owing to this spirit and a certain laziness there is a great aversion from starting anything fresh. It is allowed to develop from something else or is built up on some existing model which may or may not be suitable. When a new public office is formed, for instance, the organization of an old one is copied, mistakes included, however little fitted it be to new conditions. In the same way the railway coach started actually in the shape of a coach and the motor car in the guise of a horse-drawn vehicle. There is a certain strength in this method, for it is largely nature's own way and it adapts itself to changes of conditions. But even nature is not perfect; the path of evolution is strewn with the relics of her unsuccessful experiments. Nature cannot think or plan, but man has this power. The great advantage of the intellect is the freedom of action which it confers. If the Englishman likes to start afresh in any direction he is well fitted to do so, for although he cannot plan very well ahead, he is practical and adaptive. But he generally prefers the evolutionary method, with the results that Americans and our colonists visit our country as they would visit a museum of antiquities.

Another English characteristic savouring of the

Alpine and the Scot is the reverence for the written or printed word. It harks back to Mongolian ancestry and conditions in which a man of learning was regarded with sacred awe, and may in addition hold some memory of those *sēmata lugra*, the first writings which seemed almost magical to a purely hunting people. When one observes old gentlemen reading steadily through *The Times*, or younger ones the leading articles in Sunday newspapers, or official chiefs consuming verbose minutes and reports, one is apt to reflect upon the flippant nature of many of the compilers, who are well able to weave such webs out of nothing, and the cynicism which actuates them. There are many who are sharp enough to know that the sure way to promotion and success in England is to write plenty .

It arises partly from Nordic nonchalance that the English are a gullible people. The Nordic has lordly traditions and is used to deal with vassals and dependants ; he expects his valet and his groom to rob him ; and he does not worry about change and small matters. Out of this tradition of master and servant has arisen the division of the people into the " gullers " and the " gulled." The Englishman of position expects to be deceived. In sharp contrast to the Scot, who is not carried away by atmosphere or any false notions of good form, he considers it ungentlemanly to make a fuss ; he is inclined to take statements for granted, to sign documents without looking at them, and generally to take things at their face value. In a lower stratum of the population, the Mediterranean, there is also a tendency to gullibility, but of a different nature. These people are as a rule too sharp to be taken in, a thing in which they are specialists themselves, but on the other hand they have not the brain power to think independently, and thus they accept ready-made the opinions of others, generally the newspapers, on politics, morality or religion. It will thus be found that their views and opinions are directly opposed to their own interests. For instance they are generally firm upholders of the Conservative cause, which, apart from its intrinsic merits, is not from its origins and associations the cause of the lower classes. There are certainly other factors involved as, for instance, the lower classes favour a Conservative government because they hold that the Conservatives spend more money. They desire not to be masters or independent themselves, but to perpetuate the old division of master and servant which has subsisted since the first arrival of the Nordics.

There is however a section of the population which is not essentially gullible, and this comprises the Alpine and Beaker types. The former may be prejudiced, stiff-necked and narrow-minded, but he does not care what anyone thinks of him, and holds his opinion in the face of the world. While the Beakerman will decide on the grounds of pure reason, the Alpine, though of an intellectual type, is guided rather by morality and tradition.

This chapter would not be complete without a word on ignorance.

A story is told of an Englishman who was a guest at a literary dinner on the continent. The conversation ran mainly on one Goethe, a name which greatly puzzled the Englishman and finally, unable to bear it any longer, he asked his neighbours, " Who is this Gerty we have been hearing so much about ? " " Oh, Goethe, Goethe, the greatest of German poets ; have you not heard of him ? " " Oh, yes," was the reply, " but we call him Schiller in England."

Combined with considerable specialist knowledge there is among the English generally a great deal of general ignorance. I was amused on asking in a map-shop in London for a map of Snowdon to find the assistant searching for the mountain in Devon and Cornwall. In the same way the heads of our schools and universities are often lamentably ignorant in such matters as hygiene, ventilation and diet. Our women, whose work is of a general scientific nature, are often ignorant of elementary scientific principles, as how to light a fire or how to provide a nourishing and well-balanced menu. Naturally hygienic, we are generally ignorant of the scientific basis of hygiene. We try to bring up children healthily but regard the necessary details as fads. Many of our youths not only seem to know nothing, but do not know that there is anything to be known.

The greatest ignorance of all is that of our mother-tongue of which less seems to be known than when I was a boy. It is always amusing to count the grammatical mistakes in a political address, a school prospectus or a university examination paper in English.

There are several reasons for this defect. One is that the Englishman thinks he knows certain things without learning them, because he is English ; hence his recent defeats in sport. Another is the principle of escape from life, which underlies our education. A third is the cleavage in the classes, leading to a specialization in knowledge according to rank ; this cleavage, to which Mme Montessori drew special attention, can only end when we are all willing to use the same school.

On the whole however we are improving in practical knowledge, as the recent general strike very clearly showed.

CHAPTER VIII

THE ENGLISH IN BUSINESS

In commerce and in industry the English have made a name for themselves and deservedly, although it has to be admitted that they have had a large share of luck owing to their geographical position. While Europe has been ravaged by land wars, centuries have elapsed since a battle has been fought on English soil; and though we have engaged in wars during the last two centuries they have been away from our shores, so that our shipping has been in a position to benefit. An island placed between two continents is in a position of advantage both in peace and in war, and the Napoleonic campaigns, involving the whole of Europe, gave our trade an impetus just as commerce was beginning its career, at the same time as it handicapped all competitors. It was long before Europe made up for its bad start, and, even when it had, English goods had made their reputation.

It is difficult in this connection to dissociate the English from the Scotch, who have had so much to do with banking and industrial organizations, but I am endeavouring as far as possible to deal with English character alone. While the Scotch are industrialists and organizers, builders-up of industry, the

English are in a special sense commercial. As Napoleon said, we are a nation of shopkeepers, and that cannot be said of the Scotch. In this sense we are outside the Nordic culture, and it is here that race-division makes itself felt. The Nordic hates a shopkeeper, whether it be in ancient Greece, or modern Germany or England. The antipathy between the warlike and commercial cities in ancient Greece makes me think that the division in England in this case is between Nordic and Mediterranean ; the Mediterranean is the real huckster, not but that the Alpine is often found in the grocery business. British trade however has been a joint affair and, if the Nordic has despised the Mediterranean, the two have been of mutual benefit. Our first inclination towards foreign trade comes to us from our Mediterranean blood, and as the more risky part was in prehistoric days undertaken by the Prospectors so in later times it has been assisted by our Drakes and our Clives. The East India Company is even a threefold affair in which the organization was due to the Alpine, the execution to the Nordic and the commercial side to the Mediterranean.

The French by virtue of their Mediterranean blood are shopkeepers too and at most peasant houses you can buy something. The difference between them and the English is that the latter trade on a bigger scale. The French shopkeeper has a few articles, choice or otherwise, in his window, whereas the English prefers mass production and wholesale business. The grocer is originally a person who deals *en gros*, and this is a feature we owe to Asiatic blood, largely Alpine but with a dash of Nordic for non-chalance.

The Englishman is a good trader and a good shop-keeper, but even here in some directions he has been just a little spoilt by success. Americans are more pushing, Germans more efficient, and the Englishman has to rouse himself from his nonchalance and take stock of the situation. He has enough of the Nordic in him to assume that the fault does not lie with himself, and he is inclined to blame Radicals, Adam Smith, Political Economy and Foreign Tariffs. On the other hand the commercial man is not Nordic enough to adopt the attitude of Drake when his little fleet opposed the Spaniards. The British soldier or sailor would not have their present reputation if they were always crying out for protection in the middle of a fight. To do so is a confession of weakness and inferiority and an indication of poor racial stock. The Scotch as a rule do not join in this cry, being stronger, both mentally and morally, than our commercial class.

Protection is a peculiarly Mediterranean characteristic. It is true that it is in vogue in the United States, but more owing to the power of the bosses than the will of the people. Germany's tariffs have been designed not so much in the interests of commerce as of war. The purely protectionist countries are the Latin countries, where town sets up a tariff against town, where every man lives, as it were, by stealing his neighbours' washing. It requires the Asiatic idealism to grasp the fact that the good of the community means the good of the individual, and that the good of the world means the good of the nation, not only ethically but economically. Moreover Political Economy, especially the theory of the exchanges, is a science which requires a mental grasp more characteristic of the Alpine than of the Mediterranean mind. The ordinary business man, because he understands his own limited transactions, is inclined to dogmatize on the theories of exchange ; or, because he has practical knowledge, to assume an understanding of economics, denying it any theoretical side. But economics, banking and exchanges are some of the most theoretical subjects in existence, and a big banker works out his schemes without necessarily seeing a coin. The Mediterranean is a materialist, and such conceptions are not for him.

On the industrial side the Englishman has been successful partly on his merits and partly owing to the luck which has been referred to in connection with commerce. The recent war however has found some of the weak spots in his armour. The fact that he is now unable to produce economically as he did before the war betrays to some extent how far our prosperity depended upon sweated labour. I am quite prepared to admit that labour, in its transition state, is not in all cases pulling its weight. But one of the effects the war had was practically to abolish poverty in this country for the first time. Labour rightly fights hard to hold the ground it has won, for it is far better that no one should starve than that our trade should boom, and any kind of national advantage is unrighteously bought at the expense of one starving woman or child. Wages boards and other machinery will no longer admit of starvation wages, with the effect that certain formerly profitable trades can no longer make profits. But all trades are not like this ; there are some in which we have national advantages, and the effect of the present conditions should be to wipe out the uneconomical.

The growth of capital and the credit system, fostered by the Whigs and Alpines, led to new conditions to which the old state regulative system was unsuited. The result has been to increase wealth and commerce with little regard to humanity. To-day the wider franchise together with the trades-union movement are introducing regulative measures so that our wider activities are returning towards a control similar to that obtaining in the Middle Ages.

Our industrial products betray neither the finish of the French, the thoroughness and industry of the Scotch or Germans, nor the adaptability of the Americans. It is not that the English are not wide-awake, but a system once set in motion holds them in its grip, and they are too lazy or nonchalant to escape. They know that things are wrong but do not trouble to right them. It is probably the Nordic influence that is most to blame here for, when a business is established, the sons and grandsons of the founders, generally educated at public schools, adopt the Nordic insouciance and contempt for business. The father worked in the office and supervised the actual work ; the son talks " horse " and draws a salary. And in the bounding prosperity of the last century most businesses have become limited companies with a consequent lack of personal interest.

This method of conducting business is so easy that it is liable to become fatal to our well-being. A large company may never pay a dividend, and its shares may be almost valueless, yet it continues paying handsome salaries to ample staffs, and is inclined to meet its losses by raising fresh capital. Such is the unfortunate tendency. In the better Scotch firms however one still finds the directors actually participating in the work of the business.

If things go badly, as they are liable to under modern conditions, there is an outcry for protection against unfair competition, a confession of weakness, when the obvious course is to set one's house in order.

CHAPTER IX

POLITICS

It is in politics that the English have excelled more than in any other sphere. Here they are supreme, and the leaders of humanity. They have evolved a system which combines the good of the state with the welfare of the individual, weighing carefully and adjusting the claims of each. In no country of the world can one live, politically speaking, in such comfort, for while the social good is by no means neglected, the individual is subjected to the minimum of annoyance. Desires are apt to fly to South Sea Islands and other countries where it is supposed that the individual lives unhampered by law or convention. Those who harbour them are in ignorance of the fundamental social laws, and may be referred with advantage to the pages of Austin and Fitzjames Stephen. In brief, the right of the individual to perfect freedom implies an obligation placed on all others to observe that right, and this individual freedom spells social tyranny. On the other hand a very socialistic government is apt to overburden the individual with obligations in favour of the general good. It is England's glory, by accident and nature rather than by design, to have perfected an instrument which holds the balance evenly. To

account for this would require a wide review both of
English History and Political Science, but it may be
possible to hazard a brief explanation. There has
been no serious attempt at any time in England at
paternal legislation, no sudden personal outbursts in
this direction such as have characterized the history
both of Prussia and Austria. In fact what socialistic
tendencies there have been in our politics have come
from below rather than from above. There have
been numerous invasions of the Nordics, but these
leaders have always recognized the conditions of
leadership, namely, that they must have people to
lead. They brought such people with them, probably as allies rather than as unwilling subjects, and
their tendency has always been to foster the institutions of the lower strata of the population. William
the Conqueror and his successors deliberately pursued
this policy as a measure of self-protection. Fearing
their fellow Nordics they divided their vassals' lands
about the country, and cultivated the favour and
institutions of the conquered.

The Valley community out of which sprang the
three-field system was probably the oldest in these
islands. Later came the one-field moorland and forest
settlement. Beaker-folk, Saxons and Danes probably
followed the one-field system. The Danes, who in
their own country to-day excel in their co-operative
agricultural enterprises, appear at the time of these
invasions to have been actuated by the same spirit,
adopting the system of free co-operative villages.
Alpine in character, they would already find a considerable Alpine influence in the island which would

strengthen the feeling of co-operation and social solidarity. Such a tendency is also evident in the Saxon system and is probably due ultimately to the same Alpine influence. Conquest, resulting in feudalism, superposed a lord upon an already working system, exacting certain services in exchange for the somewhat questionable advantage of protection and governance. The important issue is that the old Alpine social institutions always remained and form the basis of local government to-day. It was in no one's interest to crush them and, in the struggles for power between king and barons, they have been fostered by one or the other, generally by the king, in order to build up a strong alliance. Out of these struggles grew up Parliament and our legislative and governing machinery.

The Wars of the Roses by decimating the Nordic lords left the crown free to create its own peerage which, under the early Tudors takes on an Alpine complexion, and the merchant prince makes himself felt, the old Nordic nobility reverting to the position of county gentry and county clergy, the nucleus of the later Tories and Conservatives. After a brief interval, Mediterranean in its character, under the Stuarts, the Alpines make their influence felt under Cromwell, and renew it with the Orange and Hanoverian Dynasties. The conflict of Cavalier and Roundhead was a contest of the skulls, the long skull, both Nordic and Mediterranean, against the short, and from these Roundheads of the Eastern counties are descended the Whigs, Liberals and Nonconformists of later days. Under William of Orange

there was a wave of Alpinism, comprising Noncon-
formity, the foundation of the Bank of England,
commerce and five per cent, and from this point
England starts on her career of solid prosperity and
sound finance.

Our constitution is based on the accident of a party
system and this in turn upon the conditions of our
Nordic invasions with their race duality, short-headed
Liberals and long-headed Conservatives. Out of
duality has arisen stability.

A party system based on racial differences cannot
last for ever ; apart from the fact that one race tends
to absorb another there is the more important point
that politics, like morality and philosophy, tend to
become transcendental, basing themselves upon the
individual rather than upon the herd and, finally,
perhaps upon psychological and intellectual differences. The most significant feature to-day is the
eclipse of the Liberal Party which owes its origins
to the Roundheads and the Alpines. Its place tends
more and more to be taken by the growing Labour
Party and our politics are recast in new moulds, but
the significance of the new distinctions is somewhat
difficult to determine until we know more about the
Labour Party. It seems to be very little representative of labour and very much of the *intelligentsia*, and
we suspect Mr Sidney Webb of strong relationship
to the Beaker type. While the Alpines were distinguished by their social spirit rather than by intellect,
the Liberals have perpetuated the tradition in a
somewhat severe nonconformist garb ; they have
specialized on the good rather than the right ; and

their devotion to Christianity has tied them to principles hardly eugenic. There has always been a
tendency to distrust them in foreign politics, and they
have always been somewhat suspect in matters like
drink and vice, where they have been forced to legis-
late about things with which they have no acquaintance. Your thoroughgoing Baptist may be an
excellent man on a borough council but you would
not pit him against a French or Italian diplomat,
nor would he be in a good position to mete out justice
as between two bookies or prostitutes. But such
people go to the making up of the world and it is
useless to close one's eyes to them. Labour is not
so squeamish, and its distinguished leaders, both
male and female, are as expert in the White Slave
Traffic, syphilis and prostitution, as in factory man-
agement, health returns or Bolshevism. Although
handicapped by certain qualities of the Mediterraneanism, shirking, dishonesty and ca' canny,
they seem nevertheless to represent the party of
transcendental reason as opposed to Conservative
tradition. For Conservatism still carries on the
Nordic traditions of the Die-hards, and is weighed
down by them as the Mediterraneans weigh down the
Labour Party; nevertheless, the party has useful
elements, also transcendental. One section, actuated
by a true social spirit, would carry out intellectual
reforms on the firm basis of tradition, and it is this
section which holds out some hope of that stability
so badly needed after the upheaval of war. Other
groups contain flag-waggers, thirsting for war and
so-called glory, or self-satisfied ignoramuses uncon-

sciously pandering to commercial greed or proletarian chauvinism.

The composition of the English people readily explains the conflict of the individualistic and socialistic points of view. Socialism is of course greatly misunderstood and is apt to be confused with anarchism and communism. All government, all human society is in a sense socialistic, as Aristotle fully realized. Men came together for the good life, and they could not come together without government. The true course of government is to steer a true course between the Scylla of anarchism and the Charybdis of paternalism or tryanny. The trouble with British government in the last few centuries is that it has not governed. It permitted the anarchism of *laisser faire* to enrich the few and sap the vitality of the many; it allowed our lords to enclose the people's common-land giving them in exchange rights of way to get to their work; to-day it goes to the other extreme and subsidizes the unfit at the expense of the fit. We may say that on the whole there is little or no governing policy or plan and, since the government is representative, it may be supposed that we have here a reflection of race heterogeneity. More probably the reason is that the Nordic is a leader rather than a governor; he has the qualities of the war-lord and the commander rather than the wisdom of the ruler. He is well versed in the rights and privileges of his class and is fair-minded enough to recognize the rights of others, so long as they do not conflict too directly with his own, but theories of government and constructive statesmanship are beyond his intellectual capacity.

The Alpine on the other hand, both by nature and tradition, is fitted for constructive statecraft; hence reform is associated with Liberalism. In the Round-heads the spirit was necessarily combative, for the Alpines were then fighting for position. With William III the Whigs were able to put into operation constructive financial schemes, and under the Hanoverians industry began to respond to the credit system and sound financial ideas, mainly of Scotch and Northern origin. The Napoleonic wars threw internal government into the background and, while the Tories maintained their traditions in foreign policy, the Whigs were chiefly conspicuous in oratory and in championing the rights of man generally.

In later years Tories and Liberals have vied with each other in constructive legislation, but the moving force has always been with Liberalism. Before the Great War the enormous prosperity of trade had somewhat lulled the activities of politicians to sleep, both Liberals and Tories being too rich to care about abuses and in-equalities. The war forced the government to govern, and it rose to the task in a surprising manner.

The socialist spirit, born of the Alpines, was fostered both by Whigs and Liberals. English character however, in contrast with that of Denmark or Switzerland, true homes of the Alpines, is of a sharply individualistic nature, and this is due both to the dominating character of the Nordics, and the isolation of their pastoral lives before they came to this country. The Mediterranean is also individualistic, for he hardly rises to a realization of others; on the other hand he has a natural, primitive solidarity with his kind, such as is found among savages and animals. It is the spirit of the herd, a kind of bond of the unconscious, enabling them to mobilize quickly or fall suddenly under the sway of an idea or inspiration. Dr Sophie Bryant noticed it particularly among the Irish.

This brings us to the subjects of individuality and originality, both of which the English possess in a high degree owing to their diversity on the one hand, and to easy freedom and tolerance on the other. The friction of the racial divisions brings into play a certain competition, and individuals go to extremes by contrast. Tired of Nordic tradition a son will break away and join the socialist extremists, or a nobleman dabble in trade or science. Moreover the love which the English have for disguise, the tendency to be always something other than what they appear, leads them to various pursuits varying as far as possible from the normal; thus a hospital student will excel in football, a barrister in horse-racing, a civil servant in golf or mountain-climbing, a statesman in philosophy or tennis. Freedom of thought too is an important factor, for it means not only much thought but variety of thought, and thought is creative in strange ways. However fantastic an idea be conceived, it will probably be found to be carried out in some obscure group or garden village in this country.

When we think of the dead level of ideas prevailing in some of the newer countries, we cannot help feeling that England owes much to her medley of races.

CHAPTER X

LITERATURE AND ART

If literature were a criterion of a people's worth, England would stand very high indeed. But such a criterion would be unfair to peoples like the Romans or Americans who have excelled in action rather than expression. As the dream expresses the unconscious wishes and fears of the individual, so literature with the other arts betrays the unconscious spirit of a people. Literature reveals their hopes and their fears, and it is but natural that its exponents should be of that type of humanity which is closest to nature and the unconscious. The more a people is dominated by its conscious, the less will it express itself in literature although by a strange exception it may do so in music. Thus the Greeks, with their strong Mediterranean admixture, rank high in the world of letters; Germany also, before the Prussian domination; for both could give free rein to their unconscious impulse; because she could not, Rome ranks low. But there are two elements in art and literature; the dynamic and the static, inspiration and control; the former is a long-headed character, and the latter short-headed. Thus peoples deficient in one or the other element are deficient in expression. The Irish incline to exhibit too much exuberance, the Romans too little.

England is fortunate in the same way as the Greeks in having the two racial elements powerfully developed. The Nordic is not a maker of literature, nor does he understand it, but he is nevertheless often a good patron. Our creative writers have been mainly of the Mediterranean type and Keats was an outstanding example ; the architectonics and moral fibre of Shakespeare on the other hand betray a short-headed strain, which reminds us that the true Nordic makes one great contribution to literature in that he at least inspires great poetry ; thus Nordic heroes are the great figures of the Homeric poems, of the Sagas, whilst Shakespeare presents us with a galaxy.

Since a people tends to work off its complexes and obsessions in its poetry, it generally follows that the literature of fear is greater than the literature of joy, for in the former the unconscious has freer play. Thus the Greeks excelled in tragedy while the Romans, practical men of action, made no mark therein. We are reminded again of the difference between the Protestant spirit and the Catholic, or between the Alpine and the Mediterranean, the former dominating God and the second dominated by Him. The Romans had little fear from the outside world, although tradition led them to toy with it ; but with the Greeks this fear, together with a dread of incest arising from a pristine uncertainty in marital relations, was a real dread which inspires their greatest work.

While Shakespeare's expression is on the whole strong and jubilant there are occasional phases of some such similar terror which may be of a personal nature, and under their influence, as in *Macbeth* or *King Lear*, he is at his greatest.

Apart from their terror-complex, the Greeks excelled in clear vision and lucid expression, a tradition passed on to the French. Apart from a temporary depression in the Romantic period the French have pursued the cult of *joie de vivre* and lucidity, and their literature abounds in wit rather than humour.

As a racial study it is interesting to view English literature from the standpoint of both French and German. That the French have a substratum of the more virile qualities of letters is shown by Rabelais and Montaigne, by Hugo, Sand and Balzac but, as happened with Gray, the flame seems to have been quenched by atmosphere, the atmosphere in their case of the *salon*. The rough words and thoughts of the peasant and artisan, so rich in meaning, so close to nature, which humanize the pages of Shakespeare are taboo in French literature; the feeling for the country, for nature, for elemental passions, such as is found in Hamsun's *Growth of the Soil*, are not conspicuous. Molière, a master of stage-craft, a specialist in character, yet portrays the character rather than the human being. The French are bound by convention while the English are most excellent in breaking it. The French never forget their formal classic laws, while the English had the advantage of never knowing them. And so while French literature plays on the octave, the English uses the whole gamut. Perhaps the most famous play in the world is *Hamlet*, which seems to break every law and convention, yet by its numerous accidentals proclaims its intimate kinship with nature and humanity.

German literature, which the student finds one of the most interesting in the world, seems to suffer from self-consciousness and introspection. Schiller complimented Goethe on his *naïveté*, and yet Goethe seems to be for ever experimenting. Goethe, a Grecian in his vision, excels in natural self-expression, yet one feels that he is always conscious of his form ; and though both he and Shakespeare had their periods of development we feel that he was conscious of them and that Shakespeare was not. The first part of *Faust* is a masterpiece of natural feeling artistically expressed, but the second part is inclined to bore by its self-consciousness. And *Wilhelm Meister*, a work of true romantic feeling, suffers in the same way as its hero—it is always being watched. Though, despite its moral tone, no poetry has ever thrilled me like the German lyric, I must admit that the naturalism which Schiller ascribed to Goethe falls far short of English *naïveté*.

Goethe probably has as much natural magic as the German language allows him. He is full of such charming things as :

Ueber allen Gipfeln ist Ruh

or

Ewig, sagte sie leise,

but German language is too uniform and sesquipedalian to admit of many triumphs in this way. English, corresponding to its mixture of race, has mixtures of language and expression, traditional odds

and ends, variations and archaisms full of meaning
and capable of lending poetic richness to a line.   On
the other hand the Germans are the sentimentalists
of Europe and we probably cannot rival Heine's
exquisiteness in this direction.

Yet in this respect our lyrics do not equal those of
Scotland : I think it would be difficult for us to compete with the pathos of *Auld Lang Syne.*   Scotland
has an advantage over us in ruggedness and antiquity
of language, as well as in her rugged, direct and naïve
people.

French literature has examples of pathos of a
pretty kind whose conventionality consorts with that
of the language, as in the poem, *La vie est vaine,* or in
the *Ballade des Dames du Temps Jadis.*   But French
shows us how poetry can be restricted by language
and perhaps it would not be too much to say that
neither deep feeling nor natural magic can be con-
veyed in a vehicle so artificial.

It has been said that Browning's claim to greatness
lies in his capacity to transform the most refractory
material into poetic form.   Whether he was always
successful is a matter of some doubt, but it is such
feats which reveal the strength of English literature
as their absence indicates the weakness of French.
This Homeric characteristic belongs to Shakespeare
and to most of the great figures in our literary annals ;
in particular to the youngest generation of our poets
who glory in their struggles with angularity.

Moreover our literary culture is not that of one
race, tradition or convention, but of many.   In Keats
we have the pure Hamitic sensuousness ; in Shake-

speare Hamitic imagination and feeling combined
with Nordic ideals and tinged by Alpine moral sense ;
in Newbolt the Nordic imbued with Mediterranean
beauty ; in Norman Douglas the learning of Beaker-
man combined with Hamitic playfulness and insouciance ; in Milton, Wordsworth and Galsworthy, poetic
vision controlled by the architectonic power of the
Asiatic.

There is a feature in modern literature from which
England is not free, namely, writing for the sake of it.
That we place a premium on verbiage is very evident
from the numerous publications which appear every
month.   In so far as writing is a form of reversion
to the unconscious it is fraught with some danger in
taking men from real life and steeping them in dreams.
And while didactic writing adds to our store of knowledge and our power over life, and real creative literature is actually creative in the realms not only of the
spirit but of the material, a great deal of tolerably
intellectual writing may be as harmful as trashy
fiction.   A good book is an asset, but a book about a
good book is of doubtful ethical value.   It is a matter
for consideration whether the numerous books about
books, about writers and about literature, indirect to
the first, second or third degree, are not a pandering
to intellectual snobbishness and to an altogether mis-
taken feeling of power and knowledge.

In art of any kind there are two parts, feeling and
expression.   Some peoples have the one but are
deficient in the other ; some are well-equipped in
both.   Of the latter kind were the Greeks at the time
of Pericles.   Feeling belongs to the realm of the

unconscious, expression in artistic form requires the control of the conscious. The former is a characteristic of the long-headed Mediterranean, the latter of the Asiatic brachycephal. The Cretans, being more Mediterranean than the Greeks, did not excel so admirably in classic control, just as the Maltese to-day can feel but not produce. The Romans on the other hand possessed control without much feeling or imagination.

English art must necessarily be considered in relation to the racial constituents of the people. We have our Mediterranean element, as the Greeks had, and it is the dynamic basis of our art ; our artists as a rule belong to the Mediterranean type as is evident from their dress, hair and other externals. We have also the Nordic type which in Greece must have introduced the control necessary for artistic expression. The Nordic is not usually an artist but, thanks to his dash of Asiatic blood and his later history, he is a controller and an authority in form. Thus Shakespeare, Mediterranean in his imagination and feeling, has the expression of a gentleman. The Nordic touch makes the difference between Shakespeare and Keats.

Then we have another very important element, usually a negative one, the Alpine. He corresponds largely to the Roman, but with us he has not the Roman distinction, for the Romans were not pure Alpines. The Alpine stifles his feelings and is antagonistic to art, and this accounts for the iconoclasm of the Puritans and the negation of the Presbyterians.

Periods of Alpine dominance are barren periods in art ; under Cromwell the dominance was destructive ; in the Queen Anne and Georgian period it gave rise to a grave, decorous and Quaker-like dignity ; under Victoria, as the Alpine influence broadened down to the lower classes, its effects were horrible and disgusting, a blot on our history and the countryside. The Great War, marking the end of Germanic influence, also seemed to signalize a triumph of the Mediterranean over Alpinism. It coincided with a great revival in art, feminism, dancing and all the more Hamitic characters, and to-day we are thoroughly enjoying a neo-Hellenism, to which both Alpines and Nordics are slowly being converted.

The artist or the singer may be an expression of contemporary race spirit or by dint of his individuality he may be out of tune and time. Shakespeare, Lessing, Racine were in time and tune ; Gray and Goethe were not. Similarly in art Reynolds and Hogarth were in time, but Turner and Whistler were anticipatory. The great artist should always lead, but the greatest may stride too far ahead.

The English cannot claim to be great pictorial artists like the Italians, or even the Dutch or French, by reason of their lack of homogeneity. But in virtue of this defect their range of variation in this as in other things is greater. Thus, though on the average the English may lag behind yet a few will always be in the forefront ; perhaps in peculiar ways and directions, but nevertheless significant. So there is nothing in the world quite like Hogarth or the great portraitists of the Reynolds period. Turner was unique, daring and inspired as is possible to some Englishmen. In the newer forms of art his spirit still informs the English ; they dive into the unfathomed, the unconventional, the garish, where the Mediterranean could not follow. For the Mediterraneans are slaves to their naturalism, but English idealism, English daring, strive for something that never was on sea or land.

One questions sometimes if the art of the Mediterraneans has not, by dint of its naturalism, worked itself out ; perhaps the Asiatic who was not an artist because he could not see has at length evolved artistry from his inward vision, an artistry of the ideal. The art of to-day loves angles and eschews curves, following a tradition which runs back through Russia and the Czecho-Slavs to the Hittite ; it is in fact Asiatic.

These two streams of artistic culture are very noticeable in dress. In a French public ball-room it is easy to distinguish the English women from the French. The French, apart from their more shapely legs, are not only fashionably dressed, but the style they adopt suits them, and there is always a sense of the *tout ensemble*. If there is an ornament it means something, and there is nothing superfluous. With the English women who, of course, may be socially very mixed, the dresses are not always stylish, for our women are inclined rather timorously to compromise than to do the complete thing ; nor are the dresses always suitable ; they are often badly put on ; the whole is often not harmonious ; and ornaments are stuck on in any vacant place.

And yet such is our variety that, while no French

woman could approach our worst, our best might equal or even excel theirs. And, in the same way that our art is inclined to run on different lines, our more advanced English women appreciate the beauty of the garish and the angular, sharp contrasts and lines in place of curves. Among the more wealthy women of an English fashionable country town, say Salisbury for example, you can probably see the best dressing in the world, that is as regards out-door clothes, for out-of-doors is our speciality.

On the other hand I recently saw a woman enter the Strand Corner House for lunch. She was small, round and fat, dark and with a huge mop of black hair puffed out widely at the sides. Perched on the top of her head was a small hat of red velvet, the circumference of its brim being about half that of her hair. In France she would not have been allowed.

CHAPTER XI

HUMOUR

HUMOUR is a dangerous subject to broach in these islands, owing to the susceptibility of its various inhabitants. The Scotch are often held up as examples of lack of humour, but this is due to a psychological misunderstanding. Like most intellectualists the Scot is slow in the uptake, but the fatherland of Burns and Barrie must not be accused of lack of humour. Education deals a death-blow to natural reaction, hence the " player " generally surpasses the " gentleman " in cricket just as the old cab and 'bus drivers excelled him in repartee. Repartee partakes more of the nature of wit than of humour; nevertheless many things heard in the London streets disclose a philosophic breadth which raise them to the higher rank. In ready repartee the Irish also excel, but their readiness often outruns their wits, and their humour is of the unconscious order. In fact both wit and humour are mainly due to unconscious inspiration, and the more this is so the better. Nothing is more painful than a laboured intellectual joke.

Books about Ireland, such as those of George Birmingham or the Misses Somerville and Ross are extremely humorous, and their readers may be misled into attempts at humour with the native Irish.

My experience is that the Irish can make jokes but
do not so readily understand them. I mean, of
course, the Irish of Ireland, who may of course retort
that it is the English humour which is at fault.
Nevertheless some of the most humorous Irish writers
have met with disastrous hostility in their own
country, and I think that those who have adventured
on humorous passages with Italians, Greeks or
Spaniards will have come to the conclusion that
the Mediterranean Race, however witty, is not
humorous.

Humour demands a detached point of view, the
capacity to see more than one side of a question, to
visualize the wood as well as the trees. For that
reason a person with a fixed idea is generally devoid
of humour, and both the Nordic and the Alpine are
apt to fall from their seriousness. Humour is a
transcendental thing which depends on the man
rather than the race ; it demands the outlook of the
philosopher. Despite any racial disadvantages however the English are on the whole a humorous people,
and perhaps the clearest indication lies in their
ability to laugh at themselves. Welsh, Irish and
the Mediterranean nations are alike in not easily
tolerating a joke at their own expense, whereas the
Englishman relishes a joke either at his own expense
or his nation's. This power of self-criticism, of
taking a detached point of view, is a very healthy
sign and a matter for congratulation.

It is a part of the variety of the English that this
humorous tendency exists, for nowhere more than in
England, except perhaps in Scotland, is the fixed

idea so prevalent. The Salvation Army is our great example and persists not from a lack of humour but from a sense of fairness and a genuine admiration for earnestness. At Hampstead I have seen an old man solemnly set up a reading-desk at the cross-roads, and earnestly propound the Gospel for a long period to a non-existent audience. In the distance people sat and lounged and flirted and admired the view as if nothing were happening. It is not that they had no sense of humour but that they respected the old man's sincerity and his right to do exactly as he pleased.

The popularity of *Punch* speaks highly for the humour of the English and, though some take this paper without understanding its jokes, these cases are by no means general. *Punch* is an excellent criterion of our humour, broad, kindly, and full of the self-critical spirit. The triumph of English humour does not however lie in the pages of *Punch* but in the tragedy of the Great War. This world struggle, when England was trembling for her existence, created more jokes than any event in history. While the Germans were inspired by the *Vaterland* and the French by *la belle France*, Tommy Atkins daily faced death bandying jokes about " apple and plum " and singing songs of a semi-ribald character. The heroism of these men was the greater in that, knowing the exact value of catchwords and causes, they treated death, as they treated life, as an immense joke.

CHAPTER XII

BEAUTY

THE racial variety of the English is responsible among many other things for the varying degrees and types of physical beauty. When I was young, Irish women used to love to come to London to see the handsome, well-dressed men in Hyde Park; for in these days the Nordic was still dominant. The Nordic is one of the best physical types ever produced, both as regards male and female, and is probably the one which inspired Greek statuary. The body is tall and shapely, the head and face oval, the colouring inclined to blondness, although admixture has often modified this character. Athleticism, convention, cleanliness and a certain asceticism and spiritual discipline have tended to keep the race strong and may even have improved it. The type is that of the dominant, the rich and, so far as they have survived the public school, the well-fed. Avoiding colds and the minor ailments of the poor, their leisure and open-air life keeps them free from consumption and the greater ills, whereas they are happily exempt from the ill-effects of bad food and the grosser forms of ignorance. Late in life they may suffer from the ills of the rich, gout and similar ailments, or lumbago brought on from excessive Spartanism. The faces of the men

are care-free, jovial, refined and bear the indelible
impress of convention and control.

The purely Nordic women are probably rare, for
in the nature of things they could never have been
very numerous. Tall, thin and athletic of body,
with narrow, high-bridged noses, they are more suited
to the hunting-field than to the drawing-room or
the marriage-bed. As wives they are dominating,
haughty and conservative and responsible for much
trouble, as many a vicar knows to his cost. A man
has to go out into the world, meets all kinds of people
and has to meet them on friendly terms. Thus while
the Nordic man constantly meets Alpine and Mediterranean men and women, the Nordic wife is inclined
to snub them. Moreover, apart from the roving and
adventurous nature of man, the Nordic has in England been surrounded by women not of his race ;
hence the old story of the young squire and the
retainer's daughter, the theme of many a romance.
The Nordic woman is neither so buxom nor so practical and homely as the Alpine, and she has not the
sexual charms and allurements of the Mediterranean.
Hence numerous mixed marriages and intrigues,
much family dissension, and bitterness among our
women.

The Nordics were a male race, and among them
the male was dominant ; attractive to women, the
Nordic male has been sexually selected. Sexual
selection however has not thus served the Nordic
woman ; she has probably repelled rather than
attracted. Man has sought new experience and
sharp contrasts, and the woman who is sexually

selected to-day, judging from picture-postcards and advertisements, is a fair woman of medium height with a shortish face, open countenance, and somewhat blond complexion—a type in which the Alpine must have a considerable share. Miss Gladys Cooper is probably our evolutionary woman.

It appears as if, while the Nordic man is sexually selected, the tendency is towards the sexual selection of a transcendental kind of woman, namely, the woman who makes a general appeal to men. None of the English racial types in itself makes this appeal. The Nordic is too snobbish, haughty and exclusive ; the Mediterranean, while making a sexual appeal, is too unsporting and lacking in character ; the Alpine too virtuous and humdrum ; the Beaker type, if it still exists among women, too intellectual and lacking in beauty. The woman who appeals to the modern English man, if he has any freedom of choice, is sporting and even daring, unintellectual but not a fool, without too much character, free from prudishness, well-built and athletic rather than beautiful, and without kinks, obsessions or complexes—in fact, apart from physical robustness, a negative type. The finished, the experienced, the noble types frighten him ; it is as if he sought something purely plastic, such as the father of the *Hampdenshire Wonder* sought for with such surprising results when, hoping to be the parent of a cricketer, he produced a super-man.

The combined tendency should be towards the positive man and the negative woman, and this indeed happens in some degree but, as it is the woman rather than the man who carries on the race, the pure

Nordic type must inevitably vanish, and the appearance of our young officers and 'varsity men of to-day seems to bear this out ; the men of our upper classes are becoming more varied and heterogeneous. This general tendency of sexual selection is of course very much enhanced by the results of the social revolution through which we are passing.

Beauty is found in the women of the three types, Nordic, Mediterranean and Alpine, but the fundamental and dominating feature of them all is the Mediterranean, and there is a natural tendency among women to revert to this dark, long-headed, oval-faced type ; in fact, the pictures of the ancient Cretan women with their dark curly hair, large eyes and tip-tilted noses are reproduced to-day, especially among the Irish. On the other hand there is the artificial force at work tending to draw the race away from this type and to evolve a negative, average woman. The result will depend on the freedom of the males to make their choice, and this is likely to increase. It is an important factor, as those who have acquaintance with lower middle-class nonconformists will realize. There the influence of the " chapel-connection " is very strong, and the tendency when I was a boy was to induce a young man to marry a godly young woman well known in his circle. To marry for beauty was considered a deadly sin, and the tenets of Christianity were invoked in the interests of mortification of the flesh. This debased, Alpine-Puritan-Nonconformist ideal is responsible for much of the appalling ugliness we see around us to-day, both physical and artistic. During the war London was crowded with beautiful women, the bolder and more enfranchised spirits being drawn into public activity from all corners of the country. When the war ceased there was a sad reversion, and we meet more of the spectacled, long-faced, adenoid-jawed, the products of an uneugenic religion, malnutrition, bad social conditions and race reversion. But there are signs that the pretty, well-dressed London girl is reasserting herself.

On the whole, in comparing the beauty of the Italian woman and the charm of the French with the average, uncomely lower-middle class women of our own country, I cannot help feeling that we are suffering from the sins of our fathers in neglecting life and the body for a problematic advantage hereafter. Fortunately the neo-Georgian feeling for beauty is doing what it can to restore the race.

CHAPTER XIII

WOMEN

DR EMIL REICH used to say that the English man was as superior to the English woman as the French woman was to the French man. After some years' subsequent observation I am inclined to agree with him. A character ascribed by foreigners to the English is virility, and it is in our men that the norm of character is to be found, just as I think that in France the norm would be found in women. For some reason, in this country woman is a variable and uncertain quantity; the strongest may break down and the weakest on occasion exhibit heroic qualities. It is largely a matter of culture, and the Nordic code has left little scope for women. It is a male and martial system and the woman fits into it as best she can. The country has suffered wave after wave of male conquest; the native women have become the wives of the conquerors, a fact which accounts not only for the dominance of Mediterranean features, but also for the negative position of women. We have no Jeanne Darcs in England, no de Staëls, Pompadours nor Catherines. Elizabeth and Victoria, our outstanding names, are not significant by dint of character, genius or achievement. Both were figureheads, and both were lucky owing to the loyalty and genius of their men. If Victoria deserved her success, Elizabeth did not, for she was treacherous to those who gave her glory. Both queens triumphed in the strength of the English-man's idealism. In literature, until our own times, Shakespeare alone has given us outstanding women of the nobler sort. Then ensues a period of nega-tivity until Dickens and Thackeray. The former, absurd in his portrayal of a good woman, excels in his abnormal and exaggerated types of the submerged classes. Thackeray, significantly enough, gives us Becky Sharp and, far from suggesting her as typical, I am inclined to think that she in some way represents our womanhood. Until to-day woman could not live except by the exercise of her wits in a question-able manner ; Wilkie Collins shows her as struggling against the law ; Thackeray in her conflict with circumstances generally, leaving us with a feeling that it was only by chicane that she could really triumph. Hardy, Meredith, Galsworthy portray noble women crushed by the Nordic code. Tess is a woman who can only be good by being continually bad ; Harold Chapin gives a similar example in *Columbine* ; Susan Lenox is a terrible example from America ; the lady of *The Green Hat* completes the series.

Scott's women are ideals rather than persons, except where, like Dickens, he gives us a real character of the abnormal type like Meg Merrilies. With Gals-worthy they seem to stand for symbols in class, racial or psychological warfare, the Mediterranean spirit as opposed to the Asiatic.

Scott's heroines have, I think, done considerable harm owing to his disguise of the actual facts of life and the problems and difficulties of marriage. Love and marriage are not what such romantics have depicted them nor are women like these heroines, and young boys have been accordingly misled. But that is by the way. It seems significant however that women in English fiction should on the whole be so vapid and intangible. In contrast to her French sister who is so collected, so much mistress of herself and affairs, the English woman seems uncertain and doubtful. She is easily embarrassed, inclined to be self-conscious, and rather uncertain of her course. There may be several reasons for this and one is her long subjection to the conqueror and more especially to the Nordic code. It may be objected that the Mediterranean subjection is more severe than our own, but the objection may not quite meet the point. Politically the position of the Latin woman may be far lower than it is with us; from the personal point of view she may not receive such real consideration. But in France she is nevertheless generally mistress in her house and the real head in the business. There may have been conquest in France, but there is this difference that in France the Mediterranean culture has always been dominant, and this goes back to matriarchy and the headship of women in the family. The Mediterranean culture is a town culture and fosters social relations; hence finally the triumph of the *salon* and the high-water mark of woman's dominion. The Mediterranean Race is feminine in its character and with it the woman triumphs. And while she makes herself felt in family life, the tradition of the *hetaira*, of Aspasia and Sappho, perpetuates itself in the Pompadours and de Staëls.

It is moreover just in those abnormal or submerged types so dear to Dickens that English womanhood reaches distinction. Our most outstanding type is probably the barmaid, for she possesses character and individuality in a high degree while at the same time maintaining her independence and retaining her self-respect in most trying circumstances. The barmaid is pre-eminently a type ; and despite her somewhat perilous surroundings she knows exactly where the line should be drawn and, to give them credit, our bar-frequenters know it also. Drinking has its conventions no less than hunting.   Conversation in a bar may go to any length but the barmaid knows as well as the actress the convention governing the " aside." And though she appears to be steeped in an atmosphere as unhealthy as can be found she maintains her standard of character, and after hours slips out always well-dressed to meet her " friend."

A somewhat similar character is the waitress of the old-fashioned chop-house. There is one near Piccadilly Circus whose head-waitress is always Fanny, though not always the same Fanny. In such places Fanny never dies, but the old frequenters of the place always think of a particular Fanny, Fanny the Great. She was dark, square of face, with sparkling black eyes. Her square chin betokened character and her lively eyes wit and readiness in repartee. She had to put up with plenty of chaff from the men but always gave better than she got, as many an unwary one

found to his cost. I have seen her hit one over-bold
adventurer over the head with her tray. There was
one oldish man of distinguished but very florid appearance, strongly resembling the late Lord French, who
frequented the place. One day he came in, his cheeks
flushed, purple and swollen beyond the normal,
almost concealing his blood-shot eyes. Evidently he
had met with some terrible reverse and few would
have dared to speak to him. He was kept waiting
for some time and his head stood out above the back
of the bench like Polyphemus bereft of his eye, a
terrible picture. Fanny was undismayed. " Hello,
ingel-fice, what's yours ? " was her cheerful greeting,
and even he succumbed.

Fanny was the mainstay of the business and was
said to make a large income and to be very well off.
She was also generous, and one heard how she had
helped many a poor fellow on to his feet. She was
of the same type as many of the London flower-girls,
also great characters, with apparently a touch of
Mongolism which may be due to gipsy blood.

Another fine type among our women was the old-
fashioned domestic servant, the one who had grown
up in the family, sober, hard-working, kindly and
devoted, one who could be treated as a friend and yet
always knew her place. She belonged to a time
before modern upheavals, and a day when the classes
were settled and had a definite code. To-day we
live in an age of transition and the servant of yesterday
is now the master. We must settle down again before
we can work out our codes.

A few words can sum up our remaining types. We

have the flapper, selfish and empty, but smart and
self-respecting; the business girl, often characterless,
but admirable in her routine ; the brave charwoman
who keeps an idle or drunken husband in addition to
a family ; the factory-girl who alternates between
steady mechanical work and the pictures and dances,
dresses well, and carries high promise for the future
of the race ; the landlady notable for her rapacious-
ness ; the hard-worked wife of the lower classes who
is now emerging into thought and faint gleams of
happiness ; the conventional wife of the middle-
classes ; the Bohemian woman who cuts adrift from
convention, dances, flirts, and dives deeply into life ;
the physically admirable woman of the upper classes
with her love of sport and athleticism, her defiance
of petty convention, and her fine scorn of intellectualism, again boding well for the race ; and finally
those few transcendental women, overtopping the
crowd, women of intelligence and genius—doctors,
politicians, actresses, writers, schoolmistresses—but
these belong, not to race, but to humanity.

CHAPTER XIV

CHILDREN

It has been said that a Frenchman, having begotten a child, considers his life's mission fulfilled. The Englishman does not take his parental function quite so seriously, but there is nevertheless a considerable variation in the treatment of the parental relationship according to racial origin. During the period of *laisser faire* industrial classes regarded their children solely as means of gain, and practically sold them. Conditions have improved with the growth of morality, but the lower and lower-middle classes have an unenviable record in this respect. Even during the war an army paymster was puzzled as to how to treat a separation allowance case in which a woman had sold her child for £5 and had put up the receipt as a voucher. There is a Mediterranean flavour in such a case for, with the Mediterraneans, a strongly procreative people, cupidity will easily override family affection, and we are reminded of Herodotus' story about the woman who was asked whether she preferred her son or her brother to be killed ; she replied " her son, as she could have another one, but she could not have another brother." This race is very sexual and, being also primitive, is not apt to connect the sexual act with its results. Hence the great and irresponsible multiplication of the lower classes, constantly adding to the burdens of the state and of the more responsible, who have perforce to curtail their own families. Such conditions would soon prove our ruin were it not for the efforts of various institutions who take over the paternal burdens and salvage the wrecks of irresponsible parenthood.

With our Alpines we find reproduction governed by different principles, although the results are not much more satisfactory. Until recently the men, governed by Biblical and patriarchal principles, would beget children to the fullest possible extent as a kind of religious duty not devoid of compensations, on the understanding that the Lord would provide. Having done so they considered that the children owed them the debt of life, and upheld this as a constant obligation on the part of their offspring. On this principle as little as possible was spent on the rearing and education of the children, and they were made remunerative as early as possible. The results for the race have not been good, either physically or morally ; in the latter respect the dominating paternal views have come into collision with those of the outside world and with the natural desires for individual freedom, with the result that mental conflicts have arisen resulting often in harmful complexes. The virility, fibre, and intellect of this race however has on the whole preserved it from disaster. Though obstinate and stiff-necked it has managed gradually to slough its Hebraic outlook and to participate, if not whole-heartedly, in the modern enfranchisement. The Great War has helped, and young men who have faced death in every quarter of the globe and commanded men in battle are not likely to submit to the cranky dominance of an anachronism ; and the force of circumstance has brought home both to father and son that the world of the future is the heritage of youth and not of age.

In regard to both these instances England has been handicapped in her social conditions, for the Nordic system has left our proletariat landless. In France, where this is not the case, landed succession sets a check on indiscriminate multiplication and gives the children a status as heirs, which with us has been confined solely to the eldest son of the Nordic lord.

The Nordic's relation to his offspring is something very different from those we have been considering, and springs from the habits of leadership which are so characteristic of the race. With warlordship another idea is combined, that of heirship so characteristic of Roman life and destined to eclipse the idea of leadership as the feudal system decayed. The succession of the eldest or in some cases of the youngest son envisages the single strong leadership required in a group of migratory rovers, but the Nordics had sufficient Asiatic blood in their veins to develop that strong egotism which always characterizes the short-headed strain. On the continent the English are noted for their will, and to some they appear to be will personified. The egotist not only dominates circumstances, but by a supreme effort he projects his personality and his will beyond the grave, and to the dominant English there is nothing more sacred than a man's will or testament. The Nordics

have found it very difficult to learn that this testa-
mentary power is only valid in virtue of the sanction
of the state, and that what the state gives it can take
away. Hence the bitter feeling of the Nordics on the
subject of death duties.

Having won the rewards of his military prowess he
has developed a strong sense of property, especially
landed property, and it is in regard to this that he
projects his will; the law of entail has provided a
continuous grip within his lifetime on the main thing
associated with his personality. He projects himself
by means of his heir, who is raised to even greater
legal importance than the living holder, so that death
is frustrated before it comes.

This sense of property has tinged the general
attitude of the Nordic towards his offspring, so that
property has often triumphed over humanity. But
the attitude is not entirely egotistic and still less
selfish, for it springs from the sense of a land-holding
and dominating mission. The landholder curtails his
own powers in the interests of posterity, his fixed idea
being his acres in association with his family. That
they should fall into the hands of tradesmen or
foreigners, men of another race, seems a kind of
sacrilege to him. And if the heir has been the spoilt
child of fortune, and his brothers and sisters have had
to be satisfied with small portions or posts in the
preserved occupations like the Services or the Church,
it is the Nordic's privilege to sacrifice himself to his
offspring in a degree which is almost incomprehensible
to the proletariat. It is usual to see a man and his
wife of high position living in a poor way, even in a

private hotel or boarding-house, spending practically nothing on themselves, because they are educating their children. The sacrifice may be unappreciated or useless, but they must do their duty, which is part of their racial tradition. They expect their sons to sow their wild oats, to get into debt ; they may know that a public school is unsuitable for them, that the rough and tumble of life would make better men of them ; but in this respect especially they are die-hards. They are an example of the individual sacrificing himself to the species and their life is in some sense a living death. It is in the nature of men to sacrifice themselves for the family, the herd, or the group, and commoner with the more primitive than with the more developed. It is nature's way, but in time the individual claims to live, to stand aside from this march of evolution, to look around and enjoy himself by the wayside. Thus man revolts and becomes enfranchized. He often becomes selfish, but on the other hand he may march on to a sacrifice which is nobler in that it is not the sacrifice of a slave but of a free man.

CHAPTER XV

ATTITUDE TOWARDS LIFE

THE English are essentially vital, banishing death from their speech and thoughts. It is only among the submerged Mediterraneans, the charwoman and servant class, that the joy in funerals and the solidarity with the dead so characteristic of the Irish, Italians and other Mediterranean peoples, is preserved. The rest by dint of their egotism are able to banish death. If the mountain will not come to Mahomet, Mahomet will go to the mountain, and if death ignores the English will, the English will ignores death. The Nordics cheat death by their system of inheritance and entail ; the Alpines, essentially an anabolic people, building up and laying by to the last day, are inclined to treat it as non-existent, or as merely a negligible bridge to higher anabolic successes.

But if the English think so little of death, what is their attitude towards life ? What is their life-philosophy ? The question must be answered differently according to the class we are considering. The Nordic's philosophy of life lies in conduct, and in soldierly obedience to command. He regards himself as a trustee, of land, leadership, principles, of a code. Whether for his own good or ill, whether intellectually right or wrong, those are his orders from Headquarters and it is not his to question. We are inclined after years of his dominance and in our gradual enfranchisement to be severe to our Nordic, and writers of fiction especially find abundant tragic material in the conflict between the race spirit and its iron conventions which govern him and the desires and inspirations of the individual. But on the other hand those are characteristics which have made history and the Nordics are the most historic race the world has seen. The system must, like all systems, outlive its usefulness, but the magnificent, ascetic, self-sacrificing code is nevertheless a subject for the highest admiration.

In considering the philosophy of life the Beakerman is not to be ignored, for it is to him that we must look for more dispassionate reasoning, and it is probably he who inspires much of our thought in this and other directions. Our more intellectual view of life is necessarily not a very bright one, for it heavily discounts any recompenses and is merely agnostic as regards the future. Such views do not necessarily lead to gloom, for their holders feel that while the philosophizing brain has perhaps advanced beyond its natural expectations the conditions are tolerable and as good as we have a right to expect. Their expectations are very meagre and they therefore do not lay themselves out for disappointments. While assessing the catchwords of patriotism, religion and current morality at their true value, they prefer to live the highest moral life of which they are capable *virtutis amore,* or from purely individual duty and choice ; their knowledge has indeed caused them to be born again, and with a soul. They diligently pursue knowledge and truth without undue insistence on their ultimate values, so that they are occupied and consequently happy enough, while not ignoring death, not to give it undue consideration except in a general sense.

The Alpine is of a practical nature and he prefers to live without philosophizing about life. Essentially a moralist in his narrow-minded way he is rigid in his views as to conduct, although his migratory ego can perform acrobatic feats on occasion without transgressing the limits laid down by his principles. The rules stand and the Alpine either abides by them or professes to do so ; he is thus liable to fall into the alternative snares of bigotry or hypocrisy. But both the qualities and failings of the Puritans and their descendant Nonconformists are too well known for it to be necessary to enlarge upon them. Their outlook moreover precludes a philosophy of life. Essential egotists, what they do is right, and they are sure of success, if not in this world, in the next. In such circumstances it is unnecessary to argue as to the why, since the answer as regards themselves is always satisfactory. The Quakers differ essentially in that they have a philosophy of life, welling up from within. Basing their existence on conduct they recognize that this is insufficient, and silently await inspiration. Thus the ego is transcended, and the eye which was turned inward in turn looks outward in a sympathetic and beneficent view of humanity. Accordingly we find the Quakers actuated by altruistic views tempered with practical businesslike experience and considerable knowledge and research, and it may be assumed that their philosophy amounts to this, that for humanity life is worth living and if it is not it should be made to be.

The outlook of the Mediterranean culminates in the *joie de vivre* of the French or the Greeks, and the fact that the Athenian women wore grasshoppers in their hair to show that they were indigenous indicates a racial trait to which the Mediterraneans are all too prone, living for the hour. They are our artists, our poets, our æsthetes in the broad sense of the word ; behaviourists without the saving grace of that knowledge which can make behaviourism other than a mere automatic response to environment. In the narrower sense of the word they have no philosophy of life, but in the broader they may have a great deal, namely, in the sense of Bergson rather than of Kant. Philosophy, especially idealist philosophy, is fighting for its existence, and thinkers find more pabulum in empirical psychology or in the chemical laboratory than in the field of abstract thought which though lofty is becoming more and more sterile. Though Bergson may not justify himself to the logicians he indicates a trend of feeling in favour of unconscious forces which may justify themselves despite anything that we may think about them. To those who feel that there is an unconscious in man which links up with a great unconscious of nature the Mediterraneans, the natural children of life, will always appear to have an intuitive philosophy of life in the way that woman has. As represented by the Greeks they were fatalistic, and in the Catholic Church they are resigned. *In la sua voluntade e nostra pace* is their life's text.

Knowing that they cannot master life or fate, they submit, happy in prosperity, resigned in misfortune. It is not a strongly moral view, nor is it anabolic ; the Nordic strives with his will and his courage ; the Alpine with dogged, plodding determination ; but it eventuates that the greatest triumphs, as well as the greatest failures fall to the Mediterranean.

CHAPTER XVI

GENERAL CHARACTERISTICS

Now that we have seen the part that race plays in the make-up of our English character, we are in a better position to consider that character generally and as a whole, reviewing its significant points. In doing so we can make comparisons with other peoples whose racial make-up or cultural traditions are different.

Thus the Romans, the Lowland Scotch, the Prussians and the Turks exhibit brachycephalic Asiatic traditions in varying aspects and degrees; the Greeks, Cretans, Irish, French and modern Latin peoples exemplify the dolichocephalic Mediterranean culture.

The English are a virile race. They are men first and foremost and have the dominance, the masculinity and the strength of the male. With the Mediterranean the female is apt to dominate and the tone of the race is feminine, whereas the essential maleness of the Asiatic is enhanced by the accident of Nordic supremacy. The English maleness differs from the Prussian in the same manner as from the Roman. There we have undiluted maleness and strength. The English maleness is more wiry than strong and is best typified by those Cockney soldiers of ours who went to the Great War and were often enough discomfited but never knew when they were beaten. They were neither like the Prussian Guard nor those brave masses of Frenchmen swung on by the magnificent Mediterranean *élan*. They were elastic with the elasticity of the Mediterranean and strong with the strength of the Asiatic. They had no ideals or illusions, they were mere common joking men, but just as painters have loved to paint them, and women have loved to love them, so perhaps history will regard them as one of the triumphs of the human race.

Wire-netting is too flimsy to build a house of; concrete is too brittle. The two together combine strength with elasticity. Reinforced concrete is, I think, an apt symbol of the English character. It is perhaps of most racial character, that is, character that is to count in the world. We have blends of Asiatic and Mediterranean in the Greeks, Romans, Germans, Nordics, even in the Minoans and the ancient Egyptians of the Middle Period; but it is in the niceness of the blend that the strength lies. Periclean Athens represented a good blend, but all the Mediterranean peoples are liable through the numerical superiority of the indigenous races as well as geographical conditions to revert to pure Mediterraneanism. Some ascribe the fall of Greece and Rome to the extinction of the aristocratic stock through inbreeding or race suicide. Something of the sort did in fact take place. The Nordic and Alpine elements, small to begin with, died out; thus the Mediterranean element swallows up the Asiatic.

An element of strength in the English is their

reserve. They are supposed to be cold and un-approachable, but the Americans have expressed their appreciation of the conservation involved in this English characteristic. The American is blithe and over-flowing and so dissipates his energy. The man who is " hail fellow " with everyone, ready to talk in bar or street, spending his evenings in talk and gaiety, is also dissipating his strength. The English-man's reserve is like a condenser in electricity. Silent, monotonous, mechanical, he is storing up, perhaps un-consciously, impressions, memories, knowledge, ready for a discharge at the moment required. If he is unpopular on this account, perhaps the feeling is in part due to an unconscious fear or perhaps envy, just as the parsimonious man is feared and envied.

This reserve is shown not only in his manner but in his dress. As he increases in wealth or power he does not increase correspondingly, as the Italians are apt to do, in outward magnificence. Rather the reverse. But his clothes, if not gay, are generally good. Fashion often decrees that they shall be really ugly, but the ugliness has some element in it of strength or quality. Garments like " plus fours " are purposely ugly, yet they are characteristically English. They conceal the shape of a man's legs, yet give scope for excellent material and lend themselves to utility and ease in sport. In our men's dress the plain and the useful are emphasized. Moreover, there is in them a special fitness based upon utility. I remember reading once of the reception of some distinguished Englishwoman at a remote German railway station. She was met by her hosts, two brothers, in full hunting-costume, donned for the joy of the thing. She was hugely delighted, but a country squire would probably have returned straight to England in disgust. In Milan similar solecisms may be observed. If a man has a beautiful tie or belt he wears it, often on the wrong occasion, whereas the Englishman wears the right suit though it be threadbare.

Here is emphasized the Nordic sense of convention, based upon Asiatic idealism ; just as sport has rules, so there are rules for every occasion in ordinary English life. If however the Englishman is captured by brigands the system breaks down for lack of rules, or the rigidity of the rules leads to comedy. We remember the story *Le Roi des Montagnes*, where a foreign gentleman rescued an Englishwoman from brigands after innumerable hazards and hardships, and found afterwards that she would not speak to him as they had never been introduced.

The Englishman's dress combines two features, the convention of the Nordic and the reserve of the Asiatic. This reserve is idealistic, and is part of that introversion of the vision which makes the inner man so much more important than the outer. It has something in it of the pride of egotism. It shows a desire to be measured by one's own standards rather than by the external world's, and we are again reminded of the Quaker's simplicity of garb and his subservience to the inner light. The Quaker's simplicity of dress is not especially a Christian feature, although it can find support in Christianity. Whereas Christianity despises externals as part of the encumbrances of this world, the Quaker, while ideally inspired, does not despise this life but makes the most of it. Like the Scotchman he knows the value of money and the world's goods and he does not fritter them away on vain occasions. And it is herein that we see the influence of the Alpine with his sound economy. It is thus evident that many racial characteristics have combined to build up the Englishman's dress.

It is much the same with his food. If we compare English cooking with French we find indicated many of the chief racial differences between Nordic-Alpine and Mediterranean culture. French cooking is elaborate, showy, flattering to the palate, technically perfect; it is like a poem, polished and repolished; nothing superfluous, nothing exaggerated. English cooking, if it deserves the name, is quite different. It aims at something very plain and Puritanical, something strong, simple and natural; steaks, red from the ox, roast beef juicy and undisguised, heavy nourishing puddings and strong cheese and ale. That is the ideal, combining Nordic and Alpine elements. The Nordic is betrayed in the naturalness, the savageness, the lack of disguise, the presence of bones and other impedimenta, all reminiscent of game killed in the hunting-field. The Nordic loves his butcher, a Conservative like himself, on account of these old hunting associations. In the plain goodness and the serviceableness of the fare we perceive the Alpine element. An old-fashioned English meal has some of the ascetic elements of the cold bath; it is not intended to be nice so much as good for you. This, of course, refers to the old style of cooking such as is found in old-fashioned inns and chop-houses. It is still the key-note of middle-class cookery. The English are essentially bad cooks, in the same way as they dress badly. They think of the stuff that is cooked as the cloth that is made up ; the cooking, like the making, is apt to be regarded as an external. And thus many a good meal is spoilt by the cooking, while some material is spoilt in the making, although I must say our tailoring, thanks probably to the Jews, is better than our cooking.

The same ruggedness is shown in our manners. They are better than they appear. The Englishman will do a good act as unpleasantly as others will do a shrewd turn gracefully. It is the action which counts with him ; the manner of doing it is an external. His pride and idealism will therefore try to disguise the action as much as possible. Of late years his manners have improved, possibly through education and travel, but there is no doubt that the English are kind, really kind, and here I should say that the Scotch are perhaps more so and even less ostentatiously. To say that anyone is really kind is to say a great deal. It means that the person has risen to a realization of others, and that he reacts to an ideal. You will probably see more kind acts done in an English town than anywhere else in the world. See a man down on his luck playing an organ or selling matches, and it is astonishing to what extent passers-by are really affected, and it is more noticeable in a county-town than in London where such cases are too frequent to enable a constant response to be made. In Salisbury on a market-day when the country-women come in I have watched the fortunes of a crippled soldier and observed that scarcely a single woman passed him by without making some gift.

In the streets and at the railway one sees constant examples of consideration and thoughtfulness, which in France, so noted for her politeness, would be entirely misinterpreted. I once offered to assist a French lady with her portmanteau on to a boat, and narrowly escaped being given in charge. Individual acts of kindness are even exceeded by the response made to public appeals, and here the City of London enjoys an enviable record. And most significant of all perhaps is the fact that animals meet with almost the same consideration as human beings.

Character has been defined as that quality by virtue of which it can be predicted what a person will do in certain circumstances, and such a standard is eminently suited to the English temperament. Yet beyond this somewhat formal psychological definition we require an empiric something to complete the characterization of the English people. Perhaps it is best summed up in that virility to which I have referred ; and this too has been ascribed to us by American writers otherwise prone to look for decadence on this side the ocean.

This virility is however not mere maleness, otherwise what I have said above might apply to those Prussian gentlemen so well described by the author of *Elisabeth and Her German Garden*. Perhaps I may illustrate my point by a quotation from Mr Forster's

Room with a View, describing a scene in Florence :
" Over the river men were at work with spades and
sieves on the sandy foreshore, and on the river was
a boat, also diligently employed for some mysterious
end. An electric tram came rushing underneath the
window. No one was inside it, except one tourist ;
but its platforms were overflowing with Italians, who
preferred to stand. Children tried to hang on behind,
and the conductor, with no malice, spat in their faces
to make them let go. Then soldiers appeared—
good-looking, under-sized men—wearing each a knap-
sack covered with mangy fur, and a great coat which
had been cut for some larger soldier. Beside them
walked officers, looking foolish and fierce, and before
them went little boys, turning somersaults in time
with the band. The tramcar became entangled in
their ranks, and moved on painfully, like a cater-
pillar in a swarm of ants. One of the little boys fell
down, and some white bullocks came out of an
archway. Indeed, if it had not been for the good
advice of an old man who was selling button-hooks,
the road might never have got clear." A fictitious
picture, yet none the less true on that account ; true
not only of Italy but of almost any Latin or Mediterranean country. It shows perhaps why a certain
Sicilian nobleman visits London yearly to see our
policeman controlling the traffic.

I saw a similar picture some years ago in the neighbourhood of Dinard. The train lines cut across a
corner so sharply as almost to touch the inner wall
skirting the road. The inevitable happened as I was
passing. A train crushed a horse and cart against

the wall, fortunately only injuring the cart. The confusion was indescribable. The engine-driver, conductor, the driver of the vehicle, many of the passengers, all the neighbouring shopkeepers and many of the villagers were soon involved in a seething and vociferous mass, and the confusion might have lasted for hours but for some English golfers who were threatened with being late for dinner. In a twinkling they disentangled and unharnessed the horse, threw the debris on one side, shoved the engine-driver into his engine, rang the bell and the train puffed happily off.

As a French friend of mine used to say : " Les Anglais sont si pratiques." Dull, unimaginative, formal, they yet individually at least get things done and in the Latin countries they are admired accordingly ; especially by women, who care little for poetry and romance, and specialize on the main issues of life. To them the English appear rich, kindhearted, practical. What more can one want ?

In Italy also the English have their share of admiration, and here it is rather of men by men. The Italian, worried by taxation, red-tape, dishonesty and inefficiency, turns his eyes towards England as to an ideal. He admires our institutions, politics, honesty, business ability and the general stability of our conditions.

Our women are not so much admired on the continent and there perhaps we find difficulty in admiring them ourselves. With the Latins the feeling is æsthetic, for Englishwomen, awkward and badly dressed at the best of times, startle even their own relations in the streets of Paris or Milan. Even if they do not wear spectacles and unsuitable clothes there is something in the misplaced ornament, the lack of harmony which seems to strive after a clash with their surroundings. Generally their *gaucherie* and bad dressing are resented both by French and Italian women, and even the finer types of our womanhood offend by their athleticism and maleness. The Italian woman cannot understand their flat figures and their desire to walk ; for the Italian woman is essentially female, preferring large bosoms and small feet.

The conditions under which the Nordics arrived in this country have stamped upon our life and institutions a system which seems only now on the point of dissolution. And if the Nordic is less in a position to lead than of old, the fact remains that the English middle and lower classes like a leader. It is bred in their bones. In no way blind to the defects of their chief, they may know that he is in many respects inferior to themselves, but they regard him in the light of an institution and an office. And although the modern spirit and modern conditions tend to make the leader more and more of an anachronism, it only needs a war or rumour of war to summon up the old spirit, and the Nordic snorts like a charger and puts into immediate practice his right to command and commandeer.

Our institutions are based on racial divisions, and have well-marked grades which make for smooth working. The Navy and Army have their officers and men, the Civil Service two divisions and there is perhaps no more satisfactory relation than that of officer and " other ranks." It is a relation in which each knows his place, and each knows how far he can go. The relation is so well-established that it is easy for officers to attend a sergeants' dance or other similar function, for the status of everybody is clear. Similarly in relations with royalty or high dignitaries there is in the Services no restraint or awkwardness on either side. One cannot help being reminded of the Mongols with their Chamberlains and Masters of Horse, positions of status, where service was a matter of honour. This touch of Asiaticism in regard to thanedom has found its way into the Nordic system, notably among the Greeks and the Anglo-Saxons.

In the Latin countries where military service is compulsory, where men of high social position may serve in the ranks, and where in many cases the officers are treated less as a distinct race as regards their privileges, a much less harmonious relationship seems to exist. Accidental in its origin and permanence, it is possible that this dualism has done much to make England what it is and its decay, of which signs are now visible, may render our position problematic. Whatever abstract right be on the side of Socialism, we find in practice that the newer relations are not, despite perhaps greater efficiency, so satisfactory as the old. The English lower classes object to taking orders from those of their own class ; for one thing they know too much about them ; the old system always had in its favour the adage *omne ignotum pro magnifico*.

One disadvantage the old system has. While unhindered it works smoothly, yet if the Nordic is cramped in his sphere and surroundings, the only way he has of showing his racial distinction is in aloof behaviour and snobbishness. The real old Nordics would perhaps be content in their native worth but, whereas the men have changed, the system has remained, and deficiencies in blood are often made up by insistence on status. The Englishman used to be snobbish towards all foreigners, but with wider experience and outlook is now less so. As regards internal snobbishness, this has necessarily much decreased since the war, not perhaps so much as a result of the war, but rather of the changes in wealth and position which have accompanied it. Nowadays to speak like a Nordic, to take a cold bath, or to display culture of any kind is almost an admission that one belongs to the class of poverty-stricken anachronisms.

Houston Chamberlain speaks of the pococurantism of the Aryan. It is not an elegant word, but it is somewhat difficult to find an equivalent. *Nonchalance* is probably the nearest equivalent, or *carelessness* in its better sense. It is the character which enables the Englishman to trust the man on the spot, and also to be cool and collected in unexpected circumstances. The Americans compliment us on our reserve force ; the Englishman is always acting, in that his real self is seldom on the surface. Among the Latin nations it is generally possible to guess what a man is by his dress and bearing, but to attempt this in England would be to court disaster. The English in manner, as in dress, cover their readiness for action under the guise of nonchalance, even levity. Under this disguise the real man is thinking and preparing. He does not react directly to stimulus like the Mediterranean, but the reaction when it comes is sometimes more effective through having passed through the conscious loop. Moreover his constitution permits of a sense of humour, for the real man, hidden behind his protective covering, can laugh at others and himself, and to be able to laugh at oneself is the greater part of their saving grace. Thus protected the soul can watch in philosophic calm and act independently of passion. It is for this reason that the English are phlegmatic, but those who saw them in the Great War would hardly bring this charge against them, although they might accuse them of frivolity. They appeared frivolous because they were inspired by no deep feeling, knowing how much humbug there is in the world, and making the best of a bad business. It is a fine thing not to take yourself too seriously ; it shows a dispassionate and philosophic nature ; the English are perhaps inclined not to take either themselves or things in general seriously enough.

English character is mainly Nordic tinged with Asiatic, and is strongly opposed to the Mediterranean or Hamitic. Control and philosophic calm are found among the Chinese, Hindus, Mongols, and Romans. The Nordics acquired this character by virtue of their Asiatic admixture whereas the more Asiatic Alpines are tinged with phlegmatism. The Lowland Scot, the Swiss or the Dutchman have the same guarded response to stimulus, but there is this difference that

they may not respond at all.   The Englishman differs
from his appearance, while these others sometimes
do not.

Those who are brought up against English character
in ordinary life become, in spite of its many merits,
filled with annoyance over certain obvious failings.
And although in England one finds in character as
in most other things a greater range of variety than
in many other countries, it is necessary to go to the
man in the street for main characteristics.   The man
in the street is the commercial traveller, the hairdresser, and the shop assistant.   Their characteristics are ignorance, self-satisfaction, commonness and
gullibility.

The gullibility of the Englishman is shown by his
whole-hearted absorption of his favourite journal, nor
is his loyalty affected if the newspaper changes its
politics and views overnight.   We have seen states-
men hounded from public life and a few years afterwards accepted as a matter of course, with hardly a
change in their character or policy.   Yet few readers
of the newspapers would admit that it was they who
had changed.   This feature may in part be accounted
for by a deference to authority, and more especially
to the written or printed word.   In England the
" word " has great significance, generally it must be
admitted in a good sense.   It has a deep religious
significance in connection with the Bible ; in personal
relations, to keep one's word has always been characteristic of the English from royalty downwards :
" Keep troth " and " Say and Seal " are famous
mottoes ; and often significantly enough more import-

ance has been attached to the letter than to the spirit. Expressed in laws or rules of any kind the word is able to wield a tyranny which would be unbearable, but for the use of fictions which break the spirit and leave the letter intact. Added to this there is a dead weight of inertia which prevents reform and progress even though people are groaning under a grievance which can be altered by a stroke of the pen. In such cases an almost divine significance is attached to any rule, and it is entirely forgotten that it is man-made and can be unmade by the same agency.

The vulgarity of the English populace is obvious both at home and abroad, and one is daily brought up against the vileness of the Cockney accent. Having no dialectical foundation like those of the provinces, it is based mainly on laziness, and inertia ; a certain self-consciousness and desire not to affect culture assist in its maintenance.

A London chop-house, or a commercial hotel in the provinces, is an excellent locality for studying the more vulgar elements in our character. The leading feature is perhaps a lack of other-consciousness, and a failure to appreciate anything outside one's social routine. Amusements like golf or tennis are scoffed at from an utter failure to appreciate them. Late dinner is regarded in the light of a sin, and the indigestible meat-tea is insisted on almost as a national emblem. Culture, education, good pronunciation, dancing, foreigners, foreign languages, art, good dressing, freedom between the sexes, are all regarded as having a certain taint of sin about them, and this is due to the cleavage of our classes, which accounts for one man's commonness as it does for another's snobbishness. It is the outcome of racial conditions.

In France or Germany people may be poor, but they are not often commonplace. A French commercial would not be startled by the mention of Racine or even Villon; in Germany Goethe or Beethoven have a universal significance. On the continent social grades — nobility, bourgeois and peasant—are much more clean-cut than with us, and hence a peasant has merely to be a peasant and can follow tradition without any snobbish *arrière-pensée*. Our landlessness and the course of history have taken the edge from our class divisions, and the shopkeeper of to-day is the millionaire and nobleman of to-morrow. We are apt therefore to regard ourselves as belonging potentially to a higher class than our own, and are therefore unable to act simply and directly, so that our actions and conduct, losing the nobility of naturalness, become self-conscious and therefore commonplace.

A great difference between the English and the Latin nations, or the Irish, is that while individuals of the latter want to know all about you, the Englishman does not as a rule care in the slightest. This feature is more noticeable in the upper classes than in the lower, and is characteristic of Nordic pride and Asiatic egotism rather than of Mediterranean materialism. To the latter the external is everything, it is his world; the Asiatic is an idealist and he is inclined to regard others only as a function of himself. The Nordic has enough Asiatic admixture to share in this point of view. His training, both as a patriarch and later as an isolated farmer, has made him self-centred and absolute, so that relativity does not interest him. Moreover the Englishman is as a rule too busy and too self-centred to worry about the personality of others.

In a Latin country the inhabitants make it their duty to find out all about the last visitor in their midst, whereas in London you used to live for years without speaking to your next-door neighbour. It is interesting to see a Hindu, Turk or Arab in full equipment walk down the Strand while the passers-by will hardly turn a head to look at him. In fact in London you can do what you like and wear what you like, so long as you are not offensive, and no one will take notice. Such lack of curiosity has another source, a minor one perhaps, and that is the English-man's idea of freedom. While from the Nordics he inherits not only a high nonchalance, the Alpines have bequeathed him a strong sense of the rights of the individual, and both qualities combined contribute to his success as a ruler of other peoples.

It is necessary in conclusion to say a word of our freedom. Its greatest practical protagonists have been Milton and Wordsworth, one an Alpine and the other a Nordic. As neither of them was characterized by excessive tolerance we are led to wonder whether English freedom does not in a sense mean freedom for the speaker ; the boast has in the past been not entirely free from jingoism, and one wonders what relation the legendary English freedom bears to subject races, to the rights of foreign states, or even to the lower classes in our own country. An emphasis of mere freedom condemns itself, since it demands the placing on all others of an obligation to observe it. Fortunately this particular prerogative is not nowadays emphasized, a happy sign of adolesence. And yet there are ways in which English freedom does stand for something ; it means the absence of militaristic bullying and, before the war, of interfering legislation, and also that the rights of all individuals, when realized, must be respected. In this sense it is based on our strong individualism, and possibly points to a great mission of the English race, the enfranchisement of the individual from the blind march of evolution, and it may be that this is the true line of human development.

NOTE—In the appendix the following transcriptions of Arabic characters are used :

Alif	a	Dad	ḍ
Be	b	Ta	ṭ
Te	t	Za	ż
The	th	Ayn	å
Gim	g, j	Ghayn	gh, r
Ha	ḥ	Fe	f
Kha	ḣ	Qaf	q
Dal	d	Kaf	k
Dsal	dh, z	Lam	l
Re	r	Mim	m
Ze	z	Nun	n
Sin	s	He	h
Shin	sh	Wau	u, w
Sad	ṣ	Ye	y

APPENDIX

ON THE ORIGINS OF OUR LANGUAGE

In his investigations of the distribution of leaf-shaped swords Mr Harold Peake has carried our ethnological knowledge several stages further and consolidated certain outposts of research. The results of his labours are summarized and the resultant conclusions expressed in *The Bronze Age and the Celtic*

World, and more particularly as regards the institutions and traditions of our own country in *The English Village*.

It is curious that ethnographical knowledge should be carried so far while linguistics which depend thereon should remain stationary. The reason is perhaps that the ethnographer goes out into the field, whereas philology remains traditionally in the study, attention being centred on the written word rather than speech itself and its users. The difficulty is perhaps best indicated by the late Professor Skeat's *Canon of Etymology* prefaced to his *Etymological Dictionary of the English Language* : " The history of a nation accounts for the constituent parts of its language." This statement leads us to a comparison of history, including of course pre-history, in Skeat's earlier days, and the mass of information which has since accumulated. Then archæological knowledge was governed principally by the theory that all light came from the East, therefore that the Aryans came from the East, that the Aryans, lords of light and power, were our ancestors, that they brought an original language with them from Asia, a predilection in favour of Sanskrit being thus encouraged. The position has since indeed been somewhat modified, but surely not sufficiently to embrace the discovery of the Hittites, of the Cretan civilization, nor more especially of Peake's very detailed account of the distribution of the swords. Peake summarizes the various views as to the nature of the origin of our allied tongues, but the summary serves to show how very obscure is the origin itself. The authors he

quotes speculate about the thing, but not of it.
Peake seems to render a distinct service in equating
the q-Celts with the men of the bronze-sword and the
p-Celts with the iron-sword men, and significantly
enough he falls back on that almost forgotten but
vitally important appendix of Professor Morris Jones
to Rhys' *Welsh People*, as important perhaps for
philology as was James Watt's contemplation of the
steaming kettle for engineering, or Newton's observation of the falling apple for mechanics. Morris
Jones' contribution is that there are in Welsh very
definite relics of Hamitic syntax, his explanation
being that the Eastern conquerors, mostly males,
would keep alive many of the native women who,
becoming the mothers and nurses of the new generation, would influence the structure of the language
taught ; that is, the language of the fathers would
be handed on, but in the light of the syntax of the
mothers.

This theory has not met with much attention, but
I have seen it severely criticized, and indeed it is open
to criticism from numerous points of view. If the
mothers, asks one, were influential enough to impose
their syntax, does it not necessarily follow that a
word or two of the old language should have survived ? And where are the Hamitic words in Indo-
Germanic speech ? Apparently there are none ; at
least I cannot say that I have discovered any, nor
do the facts of the case, which will be given later,
render their appearance likely.

Then again we have the view of Eastern language-
bringers imposing a language on an indigenous folk

of the Mediterranean Race. Such a theory was arguable before the work of Peake and Abercromby, but now it seems that the Cymry were late comers to Britain, whereas Gaelic speech seems to have come to our shores in the neighbourhood of 2000 B.C. Surely if there were Mediterranean relics in Britain they should have made themselves felt more obviously in Gaelic.

I must confess to having been prejudiced till quite recently in favour of the purely Sergian view, namely, a general migration of dolichocephals from Africa by way of Gibraltar, Sicily and the Greek Islands, followed by a brachycephalic invasion from Asia. Based on skull forms and taken very generally, such a theory is not only possible but, I believe, true. In view however of the detailed information now supplied by Lord Abercromby in his *Study of Bronze Age Pottery* and by Peake in the works referred to, we can only say that the theory is broadly true, and that the many eddies, cross-currents and back-washes now traced must be taken into account to complete the scheme. Nevertheless the Sergian view of the dual stream, African and Asiatic, carries us further in our preliminary researches of language than would a concentration on the leaf-shaped sword men. In regard to African and Asiatic man we have a definite contrast both in language and character and, though we may have to go back to Ofnet and Combe Capelle in order to isolate the types, when these are once isolated we are able to trace the characteristics of each in all the various blends and mixtures. There is a definite character contrast between dolichocephal and brachycephal, the emotional and naturalistic as against the conscious and intellectual ; there is also, I believe, an equally definite language distinction, the African as against the Altaic.

The problem of language is rendered the more complex in that the Gaelic dominants or Nordics, who brought their language to our shores, were themselves apparently long-headed, although they may have brought numerous Alpines with them. But although long-headed, they had slightly broader skulls than the true Mediterranean, that is, in the steppes of Russia, where they crystallized as a nomadic folk, they were imbued with sufficient Asiatic blood to give them boldness and character. That they were ultimately Mediterraneans seems clear from their skull-shape, which falls into a definite Sergian classification. They embraced moreover the Kurgan-people of Russia whose customs were definitely Mediterranean. Peake leaves their origin rather obscure, and it is here perhaps that Sergi is most helpful. Their skulls proclaim them Mediterraneans, albeit Mediterraneans with a difference, and Peake suggests a similarity to the Brünn-Brux-Combe-Capelle folk who hunted horses in Aurignacian and Solutréan times ; so that, in affirming that they were ultimately Mediterranean, and therefore Hamitic, I am supported by Sergi and at least implicitly by Peake.

Returning now to Professor Morris Jones' theory, we find it bristling with difficulties, and yet the numerous examples he gives of Hamitic syntax render the presence of such syntax in Welsh indisputable, and we return to the other anomaly that we have the syntax but no words. Suppose, however, that there were two languages having the same syntax, and that Morris Jones in his adherence to the Sergian theory selected the wrong one. This is precisely what happened, and I propose to indicate a language which gives both the required syntactical relics together with not only a word or two but the bulk of the Indo-European vocabulary.

Reference has been made to Skeat's *Canon of Etymology*, and this he continues as follows : " When an Early English word is compared with Hebrew or Coptic, as used to be done in the *old* editions of Webster's Dictionary, history is set at defiance ; and it was a good deed to clear the later editions of all such rubbish." Such comparisons must then have appeared fanciful, but who can say the same now ? Our speech did not fall ready-made from the skies, and its origins appear to be restricted to two localities, an Asiatic or an African. Now the languages of the Asiatic brachycephals are Ugro-Finnic, or Altaic. In his *History of Language* Professor Sweet, following Anderson, would affiliate Aryan to Ugrian, and Ugrian to Altaic but, while there is abundant evidence of influence in the way of the inflexional system and vowel harmony, that relating to actual vocabulary is both meagre and doubtful. It is therefore to Africa, or let us say the Mediterranean region, that we have to look for the origin of our vocabulary.

If it is considered how African ancestors of the steppe-folk could have reached South-west Russia, especially when their nomadic, rodeo-like habits are borne in mind, an Easterly route round the Mediterranean seems the only possible one. Any other would have necessitated the crossing of important barriers of sea and mountain, which would have been incompatible with the retention of nomadic habits. A sea-route would have argued in the first place a seafaring people, whereas the barrier of the Alps must necessarily have altered their culture. We can only suppose therefore that a large body of nomads passed from North Africa through Sinai, Syria and Asia Minor to the Steppes. In such case, what language would they be likely to speak? It is an accepted fact in philology that the Semitic languages are derived from the Hamitic, and that ancient Egyptian, although Hamitic, has certain Semitic features; among many authorities I may quote Tucker's *Natural History of Language* and O'Leary's *Comparative Grammar of the Semitic Languages*. Of the Semitic languages Arabic is the purest and most original, being nearest to *Ursemitisch* (Nicholson's *Literary History of the Arabs*). Now the home of the purest Arabic, as standardized by the Koran, is Arabia, and the purity of the classical tongue has been maintained by contact with the Bedouins of that country. Bedouin means *nomad*, and Arabic is the speech of the nomad Mediterraneans who wandered East of Suez, as it was of the Abrahamites before they settled in Mesopotamia. The patriarch, or his tribe, travelled widely like all nomads, but as I have indicated in an earlier chapter it was probably a Semitic-speaking folk like the Philistines or, as some think, the Amorites, who wandered to the plains of Russia. In any case a course of migration is marked out by language-development—North Africa, Egypt, whose early civilization is essentially Hamitic, Arabia, Syria. North of this runs the cross stream of Altaic speech from Asia—Hittite, Magyar and Turkish—from East to West.

Deductively speaking therefore Arabic was the likeliest speech of these proto-Indo-Europeans. The inductive argument however seems to leave no room for doubt.

It is necessary at this point to introduce a personal note. In 1910 I was stationed at Malta and was immediately attracted to the study of the archæology of the island so rich in megalithic monuments. At the back of my mind however I had always Professor Morris Jones' theory of a vestigial Hamitic syntax, and when I came to study the Maltese language I seemed to find not the origins of syntax but of words. Discussing the matter with Professor Zammit, the curator of the Valletta Museum, now Rector of the University, I found that others were on the same track. The Russian Consul, M. Roudanovsky, who had carried out some researches in Maltese, regarding it as a kind of mother-Arabic, had come to the conclusion that certain Arabic words were scattered through Russian, Scandinavian and even English. He suggested to me a few examples, Professor Zammit others, and Mr Giovanni Pace of the National Library, knowing of my interest, furnished further instances, some of which proved to be very valuable. M. Roudanovsky's theory was that the Arabs had come into contact with Indo-Europeans in the region of the Volga, where borrowings had taken place. As

I pursued my investigations however I found the Semitic words too widely distributed to be accounted for by mere borrowing and, after considerable investigation in England at a later date, have arrived at the conclusions already adumbrated. To show how fundamental the Semitic element is I propose to give a few important examples and, in doing so, to indicate the present accepted derivation of the words, following Skeat as far as possible.

EAR is derived from the Anglo-Saxon *eare*, the German being *ohr* and the Gothic *auso*. Skeat gives the Teutonic type as *auzon*. *Auzon* is however the Arabic for *ear*, and is known to us, with the prefix *mu*, in *muezzin*, the noun of agent, *the man to whom you give ear*. The *z* pronunciation is said to be due to Turkish and Persian influence, the true sound being *th* or rather *dh*; and it is significant that the word was adopted in an Asiaticized form. The Arabic spirants seem at times to have been shibboleths to at least part of the Nordics, and this is probably an indication of a mixture.

The Maltese is *widen*, and it is significant that, though the Arabic dialect of the island appears to go back to prehistoric times, the language stream does not pass through it ; that is, the Arabic of Indo-Germanic did not come with the dolmen and *Prospector* stream.

We have now to consider EAR in other languages, viz., Russian *ucho*, Latin *auris*, Lithuanian *ausis*, Greek οὖς, and Irish *o*. In Latin, as *Lases* became *Lares*, so *auz-* became *aur-*, while the Greek Homeric genitive οὔατος naturally represents *ousntos*.

Only in German does the *n* remain. So with EYE, the old German *augon*, German retains the three radicals of the Arabic, as did our archaic *eyne*. Latin gives only *oc-*, Greek *op-*, Lithuanian and Sanskrit *ak-*. The Arabic is *àyn*. *Y* is normally hardened to *g* and so, it seems, *iena* (dialectic for *ana*) becomes *ego(n)*.

These two words, *eye* and *ear*, are important as indicating the centre of dispersion of our languages. It will be observed that in the so-called ancient tongues, Latin, Greek and Sanskrit, the roots often appear in curtailed form, and it is probably due to the attention paid to these languages in the past that the origin of our speech has been hidden. The theory still holds the field that the Indo-Germanic vocabulary goes back to mono-syllabic roots, a list of which will be found in Skeat's *Etymological Dictionary*. Semitic with its triliteral root has so far been severely ruled out of the scheme on account of this difference. Had attention been centred on German instead, the original triliteral might have been more obvious in Indo-Germanic.

These words have been dwelt on as indicating certain important principles, but it is realized that the theory must be backed by weight of evidence and, although it is not possible in a short space to give an exhaustive list of examples, it is proposed to detail some of the most important, at the same time indicating any features of interest which they may present.

NEAR, comparative of NIGH. German *nah*, Gothic *nehwa*. Skeat gives Teutonic type *naehwo* ; he used to give it as *nahw*, and it is a pity he changed it. *Nahw* is the Arabic for *near*. In Maltese *din-in-naha* means *on this side* or *near here*.

So, Anglo-Saxon *swa*, Teutonic type *swa*. Here it is pertinent to notice certain idiosyncracies inseparable from Skeat's genius. It will be observed that repeatedly he arrives at a hypothetical type, base or root which is actually the Arabic word required, showing his hypothesis to be exactly right. In the poverty of the Aryan theory however he is forced to make the best of the material in existence, often stretching a point to the detriment of common sense ; as when, in order to connect *waist* with *weaxen*, he says it is the part where size and strength are developed ; or defines a *lad* as one who is *led*, or *soot* as something that *sits*. Thus he connects *swa* with the Latin *suus*, one's own. Now if I tell a child to do a thing *so*, I do not intend him to do it in his own way, but in mine ; giving him an example, I tell him to do it like or equally. " So far as I can see " means " equally far as I can see." In fact, the Arabic *swa* means *equal* or *like*. If you ask a Maltese how he is, he will say *sewwa* or, as we should say, *so-so*.

As regards WAIST, it is often called the *middle*, and that is what it means in Arabic, *wasai*. Is it a coincidence that Wast Water is at the foot of Middle Fell ?

SOOT was probably so named because it was *black*, and we are familiar with lamp-*black*. The Arabic is *sud*, black, as in *Soudan*, and is close to the Dutch *sōd* and Lithuanian *sodis*. From the same Arabic root evidently comes SWEET, which is connected with *suavis* and *suadere*, to persuade, for the Arabic also means *to overcome deceitfully, in the dark* as it were.

With the Arabic triliteral in view it is necessary to shift somewhat our direction of approach in etymology. Vowels, for instance, sink into relative unimportance except that as *a*, *u* or *y* they may represent radicals. English is full of Arabic words in their simple triliteral form, such as *harm, slab, stem*, since, owing to the loss of inflections, they are reduced to root-form. If Skeat had had such an origin in his mind he would perhaps have been chary about offering *nakwathoz* as the Teutonic type for NAKED. This type-form is evidently based on the Icelandic *nokvithr*, but the word is widely spread; Anglo-Saxon *nacod*, German *nackt*, Latin *nudus*, Irish *nochd*. If we reduce these to essentials the skeletal form becomes something like *nkd*, and in fact Skeat gives *nogotos* as the Indo-Germanic. This is however one of those common cases in which the English gives us almost the exact Arabic, viz. *nakid* or *nakad*, meaning " to withhold, to be hard (life), unserviceable, paltry; bereft, receiving little."

IDLE is a somewhat similar word, given by Skeat as of doubtful origin. It has two meanings, namely, *workless* and *empty*. The Anglo-Saxon *idel* means *vain, empty*; the Swedish *idel, mere*; the German *eitel, vain, trifling*.

The Arabic *àtal* supplies all the meanings required, viz. *to be destitute, workless, to divest of ornaments or goods, to leave unemployed, destitute, idleness*; in the Syrian dialect, *damaged, worthless, bad*, which seems to be the original meaning of the word, pointing to the fact that the language stream, or at least the most important, passed through Syria.

The initial *à* is the Arabic guttural *ayn* and the *t* the *taw* or heavy *t* which tends to become *d*, while the light *d* or *dal* generally becomes *t*.

It is not improbable that Semitic may have reached Britain by more than one route, not only as Nordic speech but independently from the south-west with the dolmen stream. Indeed, from linguistic evidence, it would appear that the Arabic brought by the Nordic steppe-men renewed its youth in this country. *Heifer*, for instance, a characteristically Arabic word, appears, so far as Indo-Germanic speech is concerned, to be confined to these islands. We see that with us *idle* reverts to the Arabic meaning of *workless*. The word occurs however as a relic in Cornwall in connection with tin-mining, pointing apparently to the prehistoric trade : *atal* is still used there for *mine-rubbish*, and the old " Phœnician " works are called *atal Sarazin* (Jago, *Glossary of the Cornish Dialect*). Cornish dialect is indeed full of Arabic. *Hevah*, a joyful cry raised when pilchards are bear, is also a common Maltese exclamation and invocation of the Almighty.

TALL is a word which Skeat gives up in despair. The main difficulty is that in Middle-English it means " seemly, obedient, obsequious, valiant," as when one spoke of a *tall* fellow. The Anglo-Saxon is *getal*, *prompt*, and the Irish *talla*, *fit*, *proper*, *just*. The idea of *lofty* comes out in *Tal Carn, the high rock*.

Arabic solves Skeat's difficulties with an abundance of meanings for the variant forms *tal, toul, tawil* : *tall, tallness, to do good service to, power, superiority, wealth, patience.* The idea of patience is brought out in the Swedish *tåla, to endure, tålamod, patience,* and in the Scotch *thole.* Probably related are *tollere* and the Sanskrit *tul, to lift.*

CARN or CAIRN is pure Arabic, from *qarn, summit ;* also *horn ;* from this root we probably also get *horn, cornu,* and, by a very usual cockneyism, *corner.* The Arabic for the last is *qurnah* and the Maltese *karnuna.*

The richness afforded by Arabic roots came very forcibly to my mind in reading a statement by Mr Norman Douglas in *Old Calabria,* that mythical dragons, notable for their bright eyes, were really the eyes of the earth, namely, fountains, holes and caves, whence came mysterious and terrifying emanations and eruptions. He pointed out that *áyn* in Arabic means both *eye* and *fountain.* There is a similar connection between DRAGON and the Greek *derkomai,* for both go back to an Arabic *darak, to perceive,* familiar to us in the name *Derek.*

Skeat sometimes comes up against the actual Arabic, but is obliged by force of circumstances to rule it out. It was so in his early editions with regard to the word *bad.* DRUB he recognizes as actually Arabic, from *darab, to beat,* and he explains it as a traveller's word. But such an explanation hardly accounts for its diffusion and antiquity : Anglo-Saxon *drepan,* German *treffen,* Norwegian *draeba* and Swedish *dräpa.*

LAD has been mentioned as an instance of his difficulties. The Welsh is *llawd,* and the Arabic *walad,* contracted to *lid* in the verbal imperative.

And here it is interesting to note a peculiarity of Celtic, more especially of the Brythonic group, that it tends to drop the first instead of the last radical; thus the Welsh *llaw* represents the Greek *palāmē*, and TAN, the Breton *tann*, is the Arabic *àian*, meaning *tan*.

Perhaps Skeat's extreme case is his derivation of BEZEL, the part of a ring in which the stone is set; it occurs in Old French as *bisel*, and Skeat can do no better than suggest a connection with *bis*, twice. *Bazal* in Arabic means *to drill a hole; a band, necklace, buckle, clasp, lock;* originally *to split*.

HARM is an instance well known to Semitists. The Anglo-Saxon is *hearm, grief, harm*; the German *harm, grief*; and Skeat gives the Teutonic type as *harmoz*; that is, the *harm*-root is original. It is a well-known Arabic word, appearing in English as *harem*, the place one may not enter, harking back to the tabu surrounding the deity, priest or king. The Arabic *haram* means *sin, unlawful, sacred, to prevent*; it has other meanings which it is interesting to consider in connection with the word HERMES. The messenger of the gods, he was associated with *luck, secret dealings* and *boundaries; pillar-images* were erected to him. Compare these attributes with the meanings of *haram*: to forbid, prohibition (*cf.* boundaries), sacred, inviolate (*cf.* boundaries, mutilation of the Hermæ), thief, dishonest man, illicit action (*cf.* secret dealings); luck; to go on a pilgrimage (messenger).

An important word appearing only, I think, in this country, was suggested to me by Professor Zammit, HEIFER; once derived from *heah, high*, and *fore, ox*, it is obviously neither. *Fore*, as a matter of fact, is the same word in a shortened form. The Anglo-Saxon for *heifer* is *heahfore*. *Fore* appears to be the same as the Maltese *ferh*, a colt or heifer, and in a slightly different form in Scandinavian means *sheep*. The old Semitic root appears to be *fr*, to generate, but it is generally prefixed by a guttural, as *ghaifr*, *a calf*, and *àfr*, a young pig; it is apparently from one of these forms that we get *heifer*. Compare the Welsh *afr*, a goat, which tends to show that the Latin *caper* is the same word. From the simpler form, in addition to *fore*, we get the Cornish *veare*, a young pig, the Anglo-Saxon *fearh* and the Middle-English *farh*, à pig ; the Latin *porcus* is evidently allied, but may come from a slightly different form ; compare FARROW, to litter (of pigs), the Maltese *tferragh*, to litter, and the Arabic variants *farà*, to sprout, issue, and *farah*, to have young.

HOBBLE and SHACKLE are both treated by Skeat in the same way ; he says that the first arises because a hobbled animal *hops*, surely putting the cart before the horse ; similarly he derives *shackle* from *shake*. In Arabic *habal* means *a rope* or *to tie with a rope*, and *shakal*, *to shackle a beast*, both characteristically Mediterranean customs.

HIP (the berry) is a pretty example, from the Anglo-Saxon *heope* and Old Saxon *hiopo*. The Arabic is *habb*, grain or seed, *hebbah*, berry. HOP (the berry) is evidently the same word. The Arabic root has many meanings, including *love*, *to wish for*, *hope*, and seems to give us HOPE, HAPPY, and, I think, HEBE.

MILK, one of the primitive words, seems to be an outstanding example. We want something to account for the Teutonic *melk* and the Græco-Latin *melg*. Arabic affords both in *malag, to suck the mother*, and the less common *malaq*.

Dialect offers some interesting examples. FETTLE, *good condition*, also means *rope* (Wright, *Dialect Dictionary*). The Middle-English *fetteln* means *to make ready*, and we have *woollen-fettler*. We therefore want an origin combining the ideas of strength and rope. The Arabic *fatal*, means *a rope, to twist a rope, strong in the make* (*man*), and the same development of ideas occurs in *strong* and *string*, strength being afforded by twisting.

Certain words like *stem, sleeve, slat, plinth, trunk, cuff*, open up a vista of relationships. STEM means (1) *trunk*, (2) *prow*, and (3) *to check, stop*, from a Teutonic stem *stam, to stop*. *Stub, stab* and *staff* are supposed to be connected. The Arabic *satam* offers the following meanings: *to shut; root, origin, poker, stopper, column, sharp edge*.

SLEEVE, from the Anglo-Saxon *slyf* and the Teutonic root *sleub*, has a host of relatives. Connected are the Middle High-German *sloufe, a cover*; Gothic *sliupan, to slip, creep into*; the English SLIP, Latin (*s*)*lubricus*, SLOP, *a loose garment*, and SLEAVE, soft, floss silk; possibly also SLEEP. The Arabic *salab* is rich in appropriate meanings: to carry off, deprive, unsheathe, negation; put on mourning clothes, lose its leaves, walk quickly (*cf.* slip away) bark, denuded parts of the body, tall, light (*cf.* slip of a girl), spun silk (*cf.* sleave), tree-fibres (*cf.* slip for grafting). We have also *salaf, skin, to grease a skin* (cf. *slubricus*). SYLPH may also be related.

SLAB has so far no satisfactory derivation. Arabic gives us *ṣalab*, *hard* (stone), *whetstone*, *cross*. SLOPE is probably connected, and here we have another form of the root to help us, *ṣalaf*, meaning *hard* and *slope*.

PLINTH (Greek *plinthos*, *a brick*) is interesting for its numerous relationships, and also as affording an example of characteristic morphology. This is the first example yet given of the common nasalization (compare *string*, *stricke*, Greek *straggalē* and the pronunciation of the Greek words *eggus* and *anagkē*) which seems to have assisted in tiding over Semitic triliteral into the new speech. In looking for the origin of this word we have to allow for this nasalization, for the fact that the Arabic *b* does duty for *p*, and for a Greek *th* representing an Arabic *t*. The form is thus reduced to *balat*, the Arabic for *rock* or *bed-rock*. This calls to mind an excavation I superintended in Gozo, and I remember that the Maltese workmen occasionally called out a word like *blood*, when they struck bed-rock. Related are PLANT, PLATE and the Greek *platus*.

Another instance of nasalization is TRUNK, both of a tree and the body, of which the triliteral form should be *trk*. The original meaning is afforded by the Latin *truncus*, *stripped* or *maimed*. *Stripped* is the meaning of the Arabic *tarīk*, from *tarak*, to abandon.

Of CUFF the origin is unknown ; it has two meanings, *to strike with the palm* and *a part of the sleeve*. The Arabic *keff* furnishes all the meanings we want : *palm of the hand, slap, hand as far as the wrist, hem of a garment*.

In ethical, psychological and relational words we are faced with a mass of interesting material, entirely subverting our ideas obtained from Taylor and other Aryanists. It is necessary at present however to confine ourselves to a few typical examples. SOUL connects easily, through the Anglo-Saxon *sawel* and the Gothic *saiwala*, with the Arabic *sawal*, a word rich and fascinating in its meanings : uncompactness of the belly or a cloud, to embellish a thing, to make it appear light and easy, the soul's embellishing, an image, object of fancy, a desire, an equal. These are taken from Lane's dictionary. Psychologically connected is NAME, a word whose psychological significance is emphasized in Professor Rhys' *Celtic Folklore*. It is widely spread in Indo-European : Anglo-Saxon *nama*, German *Name*, Latin *nomen*, Greek *onoma*, Sanskrit *naman*, Pesian *nām*, Irish *ainm*, Welsh *enw*. The Arabic *namm* means *nature, essence, perfume* ; also *slander*, reminding us that possession of the name once meant power over the person. *Namu* in Syrian Arabic means *to name after the ancestor*.

Trade and technical terms are well accounted for by Arabic. Skeat derives TRADE from TREAD, giving among its meaning *regular business* ; he defines a trade wind as " a wind that keeps a beaten track, or blows always in the same direction." The Arabic *tarad* accounts for both *trade* and *tread* with the following meanings : to persecute, pursue, follow the right course, hunting, tracking, package, parcel, game, stolen flocks, land, general rule, high road. Lane gives in addition, *to follow a continuous course*.

Two very convincing instances, *rabbet* and *sag*, were

suggested to me by Mr Pace. RABBET means *to join two pieces of wood together*, and has no satisfactory derivation so far. The Arabic *rabat* means *to bind* or *tie*. The usual name of a suburb is *Rabato, joined to the main town*. The word occurs in the Swedish *trädgårdsrabatter*, garden-borders.

SAG is not found in Anglo-Saxon, but we have the Low German *sakken* and the Swedish *sacka*, to settle or sink, which may or may not be connected. The English word however, as is often the case, hitches directly on to the Arabic *sagha*, to bend.

In the days when this theory was in its infancy the discovery of a regular series of derivations used to give rise to a pleasant excitement. The first such was the long array of -*gh* words, particularly those ending in -*ough*, which are such a stumbling-block in our language. The fact that the Arabic *ayn* is transliterated in Maltese as -*gh* led me to suspect something of the kind in English. The present derivations of these words are inadequate, not to say in many cases laughable. *Trough* is connected with Greek *drūs*, a tree, *plough* with *plu*, to sail, and so on ; in many cases the origin is given as unknown. This *gh* is almost invariably the Arabic *ayn*, but occasionally *ghayn*.

ROUGH, Arabic *rá*, in its reduplicated form means *rippled*, this is *rough* ; in its simple form, *lowest class of men, ruffians, roughs*.

TROUGH, *trá*, to be *filled with water, channel for irrigation, channel*; Lane gives *hole of a trough, full* (*trough*).

PLOUGH. *Blá* means *sewer, sink-hole*, from *to*

swallow or *absorb*. I think however that the word required is *falà, to cleave* ; indeed the *fellaheen* are ploughmen. The Arabic *f* often becomes *p* or *b* in Indo-European.

SOUGH, *a rushing sound*, originally *a swaying motion*. Anglo-Saxon *swogan*, to resound. Arabic *sàsà*, to shake ; *tasàsà*, to be shaken. *Swà*, to shake plants (wind), comes near to *swogan*.

CHOUGH, *qàqà*, also Maltese *chowl*, jackdaw or magpie. In the sense of *to rattle, clatter*, it gives COUGH.

SLOUGH, *mire*. Arabic, *șlà*, bald, soil without herbage. Also *slà*, to cleave, which approaches the orthodox derivation embracing the German *Schlung*, chasm.

SLOUGH, cast skin of a snake. Not an *ayn* word. *Salaḥ*, the slough of a snake. Similarly TOUGH and DOUGH, Arabic, *taḥ*, leavened paste.

CLOUGH, hollow in a hill-side. *Qlà*, to pluck, root out, extract stones, a piece slit lengthwise, cracked clay-quarry.

LAUGH, *lagha*, to utter nonsense, sport, joke. Also *làb*, to play, joke.

NEIGH, *naà*, to mew ; *nànà*, to stammer. Maltese *nagha*, to moan.

FRIGHT. The root is unknown. *Fazà*, where *z* is a modified *r*, fright (compare *Lazes* and *Lares*).

MIGHT. Wide connections as Greek *mēchanē, machine, magnus*, etc. *Mà*, to be powerful, is found as a basis of several Arabic words, *e.g.*, *màz*, to be energetic, powerful ; *màmà*, intensity of heat and cold.

More recently, as Arabic seemed to be more widely

spread than I had at first thought, I tested some of the more difficult combinations which seemed to be bound up in the theory of monosyllabic roots, and first our WH-words. This combination has, I find, almost invariably one of two origins, the Arabic letters *he* or *kaf*.

WHIM ; Arabic *hamma*, to busy the mind ; disquiet, care, broken-down old man or woman ; to hum.

WHIFF ; *haffa*, to hiss (wind), breeze.

WHEEZE, WHISTLE, WHISPER ; *hassa*, to whisper.

WHAP ; *habb*, a blow.

WHIR ; *hur*, to hurl down, rush heedlessly.

WHINE ; *hanna*, to weep, moan.

The *kaf* words are as follows :

WHIRL, WHORL, allied to *werfen*, to throw ; *karaf*, to upset, roll.

WHOLE ; *kull*, all, whole.

WHELP, of unknown origin ; *kelb*, dog.

This series appears to leave little room for doubt.

I then approached words like *spring*, *strong*, *straight*, which seemed at first sight to preclude derivation from the triliteral. It was here that a whisper of information was wafted from the " Halls " ; as people will say *snice* for nice, so in the old days they used *squat* for *quat*, *squash* for *quash*, *sneeze* for *nese* and *struggle* for *truggle* (Skeat) ; similarly I think we may connect *sniff* and *niff*, *snob* and *nob*, *snigger* and *niggle*, *snap* and *nap*. When we take into account the nasalization, STRONG is reduced to *torquere*, to twist, hence STRING ; and further probably to *dhrā* (where *dh*=*dsal*) to seize with the arms, strangle ; powerful. STRIKE, originally *to advance*, becomes *irq*, to open the way, walk in file, way, road, habit, the changes of time (compare *stricken in years*) ; whence also TRACK.

SPRING reverts to *break*, *frangere*, Arabic *faraq*, to divide, separate ; STRIDE, to *tread*, and so on.

To find an Arabic origin is now almost automatic. My children happened to speak of the Latin word *celer*, swift. I said, " Here is a perfect triliteral, let us look it up in the Arabic dictionary. I looked for *qlr* and did not find anything. Then, remembering that *r* often stands for an original *z*, I looked up *qalaz*, which means, " to be swift."

In proper and place names Arabic opens up wide vistas and it is impossible to give here more than a few examples. Whoever were the builders of STONE-HENGE, the monument looks back to the prehistoric sanctuaries of Malta, the most famous of which is Hagiar Kim, meaning the upright, or standing, stones. Is there any linguistic connection ? Skeat connects *henge* with *hang*, saying they are the *hanging* or *steep* stones, but no one thinks of upright stones as steep, nor are they in any way hanging. We have only to remember the common nasalization and *henge* becomes *hedge*, and if anyone cares to look up the fourth meaning of this word in Wright's *Dialect Dictionary*, he will find the following : " A wall, generally of granite," and the following quotations : " At Looe, indeed, the Giant's Hedge is a vast earth-work," and " They call them the Giant's Hedges to the present day." In fact, they call one of these monuments in Malta *The Gigantia*, and Sardinia is noted for its Giants' Tombs.

HEDGE in Cornwall means a wall, and Skeat says it meant a *stone fence*, and earlier a *stone*. He gives the Teutonic type as *hagja*, which, allowing for the loss of the final radical, is near enough to the Arabic *ḥagiar*, a stone, wall or fence.

Thus, the meaning of *hedge* or *henge* having been forgotten, *Stonehenge* stands for the *Stone stones*, as Hagiar Kim means the *upright stones* or, as they say in Ireland, the *Standing stones*.

Salisbury Plain is full of Arabic place-names, making us almost wonder whether the Beaker-folk or some earlier migrants did not bring the language. I will confine myself to CORTON as the most interesting example. It is a village associated with prehistoric camps. A *locus classicus* for the prehistoric hill settlement is Corradino above the Grand Harbour in Malta, the Italianized form of the Maltese *Cordin* or *Kortin*. Its diminutive is *Cretin*, found in Malta both as a place-name and as a proper-name, *Cretien*. This broken diminutive is found in *Credenhill*, a prehistoric station in Herefordshire. The word is naturally widespread : Welsh *Garthęn*, at present derived from *caer*, a fortified enclosure, and *din*, a fortified hill ; *Gortyn* (Crete), *Cortona* (Italy), *Cortina* (Tyrol), *Cordenn* (Brittany) and possibly *Gordon* (Scotland) ; also probably in the Irish *cruith*, a little eminence, and *cruithin*, a hump on the back, both apparently from the diminutive form.

The word has the puzzling appearance of a compound, and compounds of this type are rare in Arabic. *Qarr, to dwell*, and *din, town* (as in the derivative *Medina*), suggest themselves, but they do not seem convincing. Taylor however is illuminating on the subject : " There is a considerable doubt whether *caer* is a modification of *castra*, or an independent Celtic root. We have the British and Cornish *caer*, the Armorican *ker*, and the Irish *cathair* or *ca'ir*, a fortress, and the Welsh *cae*, an enclosure, and *cor*, a close. Compare the Hebrew and Phœnician word *kartha*, which is seen in the names Kerjath, Kerioth, Kir and Carthage, and is identical in meaning with the Celtic *caer*. If there is no affiliation this is a very remarkable coincidence of sound and meaning " (*Names and Places*).

When we come to consider CURTAIN, originally a *bastion* or *the curtain of a castle*, we find it derived from Low Latin *cortina*, a small court or enclosure, curtain of a castle. This Skeat derives from *cohortem* and associates it with *hortus, garth, yard* and *garden*. These last seem to be allied to the Phœnician *kartha*, and perhaps *kortin* is a derivative form, a plural, or more likely a diminutive, parallel to the Low Latin *cortina*.

Mr Peake says Rome was built by the terramara refugees fleeing before the Nordic steppe-folk, and that they called the PALATINE from their town of Palatium. Both words, as also the Greek *polis*, are from the Arabic *balad*, a town. The Maltese always know their capital, not as Valletta, but as *il Belt*.

And who is PALLAS ATHENE ? We know how in old days the tutelary deities were identified with their cities, and *Pallas* is accounted for above. What is Athene's distinction ? Her name has been impossibly associated with flowers and other things, but we remember that when Poseidon gave the horse to man, she gave the olive. If hers is the town of olives, what would be its name ? Wherever Arabic is spoken there are olive-towns, and their name is *Zeitun*, the Arabic for *olives*. The town of olives would be more fully *balad zeitun*, which by a common wrong division seems to have become *baladz eitun*, or *Pallas Athene*.

It is impossible here to deal adequately with place-names, but those of our rivers have been suggested by various writers as containing the elements of primitive speech in our islands. Canon Taylor in *Names and Places* suggests the following as inviting investigation. I give them with the Arabic : NEATH, *nath*, to ooze, moist ; SOAR, *sūr*, strong, to rush ; MAY, *ma*, water ; DEE, *dawa*, to echo ; TEES, *tās*, to dash together ; CHAR, *jarr*, brook ; KEN, *kin*, hidden ; LEA, *lawa*, to twist.

There is a whole set of river-names in THAMES, TAM, TAMAR, TAME and TEME, of which Skeat can find no origin. Johnston (*Place-Names of England and Wales*) says they are allied to the Gaelic *tamh*, rest ; Taylor suggests the Celtic *tam*, spreading. A common Arabic root, *iam*, runs through the following : *iam*, to overwhelm, mass of water ; *iamah*, to swell ; *iamar*, to swell ; *iames*, to sink into water, blot out. For TAFF and TAVY we have *iaf*, to overflow.

That must suffice for examples. It may be asked how much of the Indo-Germanic vocabulary is so far covered by Arabic derivations. At present I have a large number of instances and, although they are not exhaustive, there are few classes of words which do not ultimately yield to the Semitic test. My examples cover practically all the parts of the body, most domestic, technical, relational and psychological words, and many pronouns and particles. Numerals are at least partly covered, and words of parentage fairly adequately. Here however much mutilation must have taken place. The important point emerges that the bulk of primitive Indo-European words appear to be Semitic.

The theory was first worked out on the hypothesis of a people of the Mediterranean Race being in possession of Europe at the time of the infiltration of brachycephals from Asia, who adopted the language of the indigenous people. It is difficult to discard this view altogether; it is equally difficult to gainsay Mr Peake's main conclusions. Possibly for the present we may compromise in this way: the first steppe-folk were originally Mediterraneans and brought an Arabic language to Europe; they mixed with Asiatics and, on adopting a career of conquest, were accompanied by numerous short-headed Alpines. Now the true language of the Asiatic brachycephal appears to be some form of Ugro-Finnic or Altaic. A certain adjustment between this and Semitic seems to have taken place. The strange consonantal mutations of the Celtic languages point to Urgo-Finnic influences, whereas Professor Sweet in his *History of Languages* is inclined to trace the Indo-Germanic inflexional and morphological system to an Ugrian and finally to an Altaic source: " Just as Ugrian shows a stage of inflection out of which the Aryan inflections would naturally develop, so also Altaic shows a state of agglutination out of which, as shown in Turkish, such inflections as we find in Ugrian not only could, but almost invariably must have developed."

The syntax which Morris Jones found in Welsh is not Hamitic so much as Arabic ; in some cases the very words he gives are Arabic. The Celtic languages are full of Arabic turns of expression : in both Irish and Welsh " the woman of the house " takes the form " woman the house," as in Arabic.

The position as envisaged by Professor Morris Jones is however curiously reversed. Instead of the Indo-Germanic languages being something with Hamitic syntax traces, they appear to be mainly Arabic with Altaic inflections and formative system. What exactly happened it is difficult at present to surmise. There were difficulties in pronouncing the Arabic *th*, *sh* (which became *sc* and then again *sh*) and *dh* (as in *auzon*) ; but in English we find a reversion in these matters to pure Arabic. The speech of the Celtic wanderers to our islands became mutilated by Ugro-Finnic influences, which are not found in the more original Latin—I mean the Celtic aspirations and consonantal changes. With the Germanics a similar purity is found, but even here the pronunciation of *th* is not Arabic as it is in English. These Celtic corruptions in our islands are due to some special cause, and this is probably to be found in the pre-Nordic Maglemosian stream from Scandinavia, whereas the comparative purity of English may be due to another Arabic stream from the South-west, in which the language refreshed itself.

There were doubtless other language streams, and

one purely Berber or Hamitic found its way into Basque, which contains numerous Hamitic words overlaid by an Ugro-Finnic system. I have personally discovered many of these Hamitic words in Basque and find that Professor Sayce confirms this. Here we must have a stream from Africa direct without passing through the Semitic loop and possibly prior to the Arabic stream.

The field is naturally a very large one, involving a complete overhaul of our etymology, and it is hoped that the large amount of data I have so far collected may be of use for further investigation of an interesting problem.

INDEX